Endorsements for Hurricane of Love

"I have been a fan of Dan Wheeler's work on TV for a long time. But I must say that his work as an author is a gift to all of us. *Hurricane of Love* is a heartfelt and touching tribute to his wife Beth. This is a "must read" book of hope and inspiration!

Jay Sekulow, Chief Counsel, American Center for Law & Justice, Counsel to the 45th President of the United States

"Hurricane of Love" is a blessing. More importantly, this book is an encouragement and an invitation to live life in the moment. I know, as a part of Beth and Dan's purpose-driven journey, that the story of her battle and their deep love will bless you and help you, as it has me, persevere through any adversity. Read this book!"

John Tesh, Composer, Musician, Nationally syndicated Radio-TV host

"This book is a great tribute to Beth Wheeler who I knew and loved for 27 years. Her spirit and love for Jesus radiated in her constant smile, her giggle, and in the way she loved her family and friends. I praise God He allowed us to share such a wonderful friendship."

Mary Beth Roe, QVC Host

"I worked with Dan on QVC many times while his wife, Beth, was battling cancer. I saw how their faith in the Lord gave them the strength to keep going. This book is a story of faith and hope that will inspire you no matter where you are or what you are facing. Read this book!"

Mike Lindell, Inventor/CEO MyPillow

"With an inspiring combination of humor, candor and complete vulnerability, Dan Wheeler bares his soul in *Hurricane of Love*. It's a spiritual journey and one you'll never forget!"

Rick Domeier, QVC Host and author of *Can I Get a DO OVER*

Hurricane of
of

Love

My Journey with Beth Wheeler

Dan Wheeler

WESTBOW
PRESS®
A DIVISION OF THOMAS NELSON
& ZONDERVAN

WestBow Press books may be ordered through booksellers or by contacting:

WestBow Press
A Division of Thomas Nelson & Zondervan
1663 Liberty Drive
Bloomington, IN 47403
www.westbowpress.com
1 (866) 928-1240

Scripture taken from the King James Version of the Bible.

ISBN: 978-1-9736-3290-0 (sc)
ISBN: 978-1-9736-3289-4 (hc)
ISBN: 978-1-9736-3291-7 (e)

Library of Congress Control Number: 2018907709

Printed in the United States.

WestBow Press rev. date: 8/10/2018

To Beth, who taught us all how to love.

Contents

Preface

The title of this book perfectly describes my late wife, Beth. I didn't come up with the phrase "Hurricane of Love." My niece, Terra, did. She has a wonderful way with words. The day before Beth left this earth, Terra wrote in her blog, "My aunt Beth's love was like a hurricane. It hit everyone in its path."

I said, "Terra, that is the perfect way to describe it. If you don't mind, that will be the title of Beth's biography. *Hurricane of Love: My Journey with Beth Wheeler.*"

My wife, Elizabeth (Beth) Ann Wheeler had an extraordinary gift. Within minutes of meeting her, people felt as if they had known her all their lives. She had this enviable ability to make everyone feel instantly comfortable, like they belonged. She treated every visitor to our home as if they were family. If anyone ever thrived on making people feel good about themselves it was Beth Wheeler.

Many of our daughters' friends considered her their second mom. I know well over a dozen people who thought of Beth as their "very best friend." She was true blue and never betrayed a confidence. She loved deeply and overflowed with kindness. I am one of those people who considered her my best friend. I am the lucky guy who was married to her, for almost thirty-one years.

Beth was joyful, but more importantly, she was content. From time to time, I would ask her what her dreams and goals were. My favorite question was, "If you could do anything with your life what would you do?"

Her answer never changed. She always responded, "I'm doing it! I always wanted to be a mom and a wife, and I am so blessed to be both."

Beth never sought to be rich and famous, but she felt like she was more affluent than the wealthiest person in the world and she was a superstar to everyone who knew her.

In October of 2012, my wife was diagnosed with stage 4 Endometrial Cancer. With that diagnosis, our lives changed in an instant. But my wife's attitude toward life never changed. She had a strong will to live and fought with everything she had. Her joy and care for others remained strong throughout her battle.

In the final weeks of her life, I asked if I could post about our journey on Facebook. I told her that I thought we could help a lot of people who were facing a similar battle. I had never posted anything about her condition up to this point, so my Facebook followers had no idea what we were going through. She told me that she trusted me to write whatever I felt God was laying on my heart.

Because I was a host on QVC at the time, thousands of people read my posts. When I started posting about Beth's battle with cancer, hundreds of thousands of people began reading them. People were following our journey around the world. My daughter, Kelsey, received a text from a friend in Connecticut one day telling her that the stylists and customers at her hair salon were all talking about Beth Wheeler.

Her Celebration of Life Service was "live streamed" from our church, Calvary Fellowship Downingtown, on November 3rd, 2015. Thousands of people watched it online that day, and tens of thousands have viewed it since on YouTube. I have heard from people around the world telling me that service positively impacted their lives. Hundreds of people wrote to say that they wished they could have known Beth Wheeler on earth, and they look forward to meeting her someday in heaven.

If you are currently battling a life-threatening illness or helping a loved one who is facing a severe health challenge, I hope that you win that battle. I pray our story fills you with hope and faith. Know that God will be with you every step of the way. He walked beside us, and at times, carried us throughout this journey.

If you have recently lost a loved one, then I hope our story will fill you with the peace, comfort, and hope that only God can bring.

After Beth passed, many people told me I should write a book about her life and our journey. Here it is. I hope that after reading this book, you will have a strong sense of who Beth Wheeler was. I am confident that once you do, you will love her too. More importantly, I hope you will be inspired by her life and her faith in Jesus Christ. She only lived sixty-one years, but oh how she lived! Everyone dies, but many never really live. Beth lived every day to its fullest.

My primary goal in writing this book is for you to get to know this extraordinary woman. I believe that by the end of this book, you will look forward to meeting her in heaven. She loved her life and all those who were in it. She inspired us all to love more deeply and unconditionally.

I have worked on national television for more than thirty years, but it is now time to put the spotlight on the real star of the Wheeler family.

Acknowledgements

Writing a book is a major undertaking but this book was an extra challenge for me because of all of the emotions involved. It felt like I was chiseling a sculpture with a small chisel: bit by bit and emotion after emotion. It was difficult at times to relive Beth's final years but it was cathartic. Finally, the book is finished and I can move forward. I have many people to thank who helped me complete the task of this tribute to my late wife, Beth Wheeler.

First, I would like to thank my family. To my daughters, Kirstyn Hauser and Kelsey Wheeler, thank you for caring for and loving your mom intensely and for helping me so much during mom's three- year battle with cancer. Mom and I are so proud of the women you have become. Thanks for writing such beautiful tributes to her. I want to thank Beth's mom, Elaine Johnson, for raising such an amazing daughter. My son-in-law, Jeff Hauser, went above and beyond to help and support Kirstyn as she cared for Beth. Cole, Gavin and Brooke you add so much to Papa's life. Thank you for every hug and every kiss. I'd like to thank Jeff's parents, Ed and Nancy Hauser, and the entire Hauser family for their love and support along our journey.

QVC is the best company in the world and I am so grateful for the amazing people there who comforted and strengthened me during the tough times. My fellow hosts were amazing in filling in for me on air when I needed to be with Beth during her final days. I am forever grateful to you all for giving me the gift of precious time to be with her during her final days. The entire QVC Talent department deserves my thanks including our leader, Jack Comstock, Caroline Stueck, Mary Harlyvetch and Mary Ricks.

Sharon Hanby-Robie you have been a dear friend to me over the years and I can't thank you enough for lending your writing/ editing expertise to this project "free of charge." Your feedback was invaluable and got me going in the right direction!

To my editor, Jaxn Hill, thank you for taking on this project with such short notice. You are the best and you made this book the best it could be.

To Bryan Law, who built a ramp to transport Beth in and out of the house at the end with an hour's notice and to Oscar Dovale who put in many selfless hours on the beautiful video that honored Beth's life, I say thank you from the bottom of my heart for showing me true "love in action."

I would like to thank my team at West Bow Press. Deanna George thanks for your friendship and support. You are the reason I went with West Bow Press in the first place. Thanks to Selina McCarty –Doughty for keeping me posted during Deanna's brief absence. Thanks to Ric Basso, the Publishing Sales Manager at West Bow Press for getting behind this project. Lisa McCarthy, thanks so much for helping to get the word out and Venus Gamboa thanks for keeping me on track!

I owe a debt of gratitude to Jay Sekulow and his family for reaching out to me as I was leaving QVC and for supporting Fearless Faith. You are a seriously busy guy and I am so appreciative of your time and friendship. Thank you for giving me your thoughtfully written endorsement. Another big thanks goes to John Tesh for your help, endorsement and friendship through the years. I'll never forget working with you on "The Dawn of the New Millenium" from Gisborne, New Zealand.

Mike Lindell, thank you for all of your support for me and Fearless Faith and your great endorsement of this book. To my dear friends and fellow QVC hosts Mary Beth Roe and Rick Domeier I say, "Thanks for your endorsement and for loving my family all these years." You both define "friendship." To my teammates and friends at Fearless Faith. Brian Roland, Terry Steen and Silvia Aronson, thanks for your undying friendship and support and for contributing your amazing talents to this book. Silvia, thank you for all of your professional work on the photos. You made them the best they could be. Thank you for pulling me through!

I want to give extra credit to the photographers who provided the images in this book. The cover photo is courtesy of Jensen Photography as are a couple interior shots of my family. Kirstyn's wedding pictures are courtesy of Duca Studio and the amazing shot of my three grandchildren is courtesy of Kealy Creative. Oscar Dovale took the Author's photo. Thanks to Roy Johnson and Carol Bellone for helping me find pictures of your sister.

Finally, to the QVC viewers who have always shown me so much love. Thanks for the tens of thousands of messages of encouragement and support. You have no idea how much every message and every kind word meant to me during Beth's final days and all the days since then. God bless you all!

Introduction

"In the day of prosperity be joyful, but in the day of adversity consider: God also set the one over against the other, to the end that man should find nothing after him."-Ecclesiastes 7:14, The Bible, King James Version

When Beth and I were dating in the late 1970's, we occasionally took weekend trips from Chicago to South Haven, Michigan to visit my dad, Joe, and his wife, Sally. My grandparents, who were in their late 70's at the time, lived nearby, so we usually stopped in to say hello.

On more than one occasion, we walked into their quaint two-bedroom home and were greeted by the sound of laughter. We usually discovered they were in the middle of a game of *Parcheesi* with their neighbors, who were around the same age. We were amazed at how much joy they found in a simple board game.

It made Beth and me decide that we wanted to grow old together and play *Parcheesi*. A few years later, when I asked her to marry me, I put the engagement ring inside the box of a *Parcheesi* game. As soon as she saw the box, she knew what it meant.

I regret that in our almost thirty-one years of marriage, we didn't play enough *Parcheesi*. However, we did live out a fantastic love story. We raised two beautiful daughters and became very proud grandparents.

During the last three years of Beth's life, we went on a profoundly life-changing and challenging journey. It was a journey that went directly through "the valley of the shadow of death." All of our priorities were turned upside down, but ultimately right side up. I learned that truly loving someone means taking care of that person in sickness as well as in health. I had a front row seat to an incredible display of faith, courage, and grace in the face of death.

You are about to take that journey with me. You will read about many "coincidences" that I believe were miracles. Some were dramatic, while others were more commonplace. They all arrived at the precise time that we needed them. They were signs that let me know that God was still with us even in our darkest hours. The most significant miracle of all, however, was the unconditional love God showed me through my wife, Beth Wheeler. I'm so grateful for the wonderful life we had and the beautiful family we raised.

The final three years of our life together were almost unbearable at times. You will read about the stress that I experienced in my dual roles as the host of live television shows on QVC and primary caregiver for my very sick wife at home. I thank God I worked for such an excellent company that supported me every step of the way.

Looking back now, I realize that even though sorrow and pain filled the final years, deep meaning and God's love filled them, too. God was faithful through it all, and I am a much better man for having gone through it.

At certain places in this book, I offer you advice based on what I experienced. That advice, along with scripture references, is in bold typeface because I don't want you to miss the message.

I spent thirty-seven years of my life with Beth Ann Wheeler. We had been married for almost thirty-one when God took her home. I am beyond thankful for every minute we had together. I only wish we could have had more time to spend together. I would have liked for us to play a little more *Parcheesi*.

Somewhere early in our dating life, Beth and I started calling each other "Baby Cakes," which later evolved into "Cakies." I hope you enjoy getting to know my Cakies, but I have to warn you: her love IS like a hurricane. It hits everyone in its path. Be prepared!

1

$\mathcal{T}$hey're Going to Tell
Me I Have Cancer!

Beth began complaining of stomach pain during the summer of 2012. She described the pain by saying it felt like the Pac Man character (from the video game) was eating away at the lining of her stomach. I begged her to go to the doctor. I was startled when she said, "I don't want to go to the doctor because she is just going to tell me I have cancer!"

You can imagine my response: "PLEASE GET TO THE DOCTOR NOW!!!"

She drove back to the Chicago area to spend some time with her sister, Carol, her brother, Roy, and her mom, Elaine, in early September of that year. She and her siblings were helping their eighty-seven-year-old mom go through her belongings to rid her condo of some of the clutter that had built up over the years. I remember talking to her on the phone while she was there. She told me that her stomach pain was getting worse. We agreed that as soon as she got home, she would make an appointment with her doctor. Once again she said, "They will just tell me I have cancer." When she made the call to her doctor's office, they told her their first opening was over two weeks away.

I worked for the multichannel electronic retailer QVC as an on-air television host at the time. I was in and out of meetings at

QVC Studio Park on Friday, October 19th, 2012. I checked my messages around 1 p.m. and discovered I had several texts and voice messages from Beth saying, "Call me immediately!" and then, "Please come home now!!!" When I called her, she told me her doctor believed she might have cancer. I'll never forget that moment. My world instantly turned upside down.

I ran out of QVC's headquarters in West Chester, Pennsylvania and drove home as fast as I could. When I walked into our house, I found Beth sitting on our bed hugging a pillow. It was evident that she had been crying a lot.

I sat down next to her, and asked her what the doctor said. Beth told me, "As the nurse was doing my ultra-sound she kept saying that she didn't like what she was seeing. She told me my uterine wall was too thick, and it looked like cancer. As I was driving home, the doctor called and said I needed to come back right away because they needed to get a biopsy."

I threw my arms around her and told her everything would be ok. "We'll get through this together with the Lord's help," I said emphatically. But I was terrified. Fear gripped my heart, and my head felt like it was in a vice that someone kept tightening. In times like this, we tend to panic before we pray. But on this day, Beth and I began praying right away. We prayed and hugged each other well into the evening. Beth told me she didn't want to die. She wanted to be around to watch our family continue to grow and to grow old together with me.

That was one of the longest weekends of my life. The future was uncertain, but I was confident that God held it in His hands. The following Wednesday, we got the call confirming the biopsy was malignant.

Beth had cancer, and we had a million questions with no answers. What kind of cancer? Where was it? How much had it spread? What can be done to treat it? The list went on and on and on. I kept assuring Beth that everything was going to be ok, and that I would be with her every step of the way. I had no idea how difficult the next three years would be, or how steep the mountain was that we were about to climb.

Our first challenge was figuring out how to break the news to our daughters. Our oldest daughter, Kirstyn, is a registered nurse. I remember how surprised we were when half way through her college career she said that she wanted to change her major from elementary education to nursing. God wasn't surprised. He knew how important that decision would be for our family.

Kirstyn had been married for two years, and had one young son at the time of Beth's diagnosis. Fortunately, she lived just fifteen minutes away. Our youngest daughter, Kelsey, was a sophomore at Messiah College, which is located about an hour and a half away from our home by car.

Beth broke the news to Kirstyn on Thursday. When she heard that her mom had cancer, she was upset, and then almost immediately put on her nursing hat and started planning our course of action. She told Beth that our first goal was to find the very best cancer doctor around.

Beth called Kelsey and asked her to come home for the weekend to celebrate my birthday on Friday, October 26th. When she walked into the house, we sat her down and told her that her mommy had cancer. She immediately looked at Beth and asked, "Are you going to die?" Kelsey is always direct and to the point. Even though I told her that her mom was not going to die, that was the question on all of our minds. At this point, we had no idea where the cancer was, and how much it had spread. Kelsey verbalized what we were all wondering but were afraid to admit.

You never want to be in a position to hire a lawyer or an oncologist—but if you do, you want the very best. We wanted the very best cancer surgeon we could find, so we wasted no time in the search, and the following week we interviewed a surgeon at our local hospital. Unfortunately, none of us came out of that interview with a good feeling.

We decided to look into the Oncology Department at a large, well-respected hospital in Philadelphia. Beth and Kirstyn went right to the top and called the head of the Gynecologic/Oncology department and, miraculously got an appointment for the following week. I'm going to call him Dr. John (not his real name). He was known as "the man with the golden hands" because of his tremendous surgical skills. After reviewing Beth's ultrasound, he scheduled surgery for two weeks later on November 14, 2012.

The Bible tells us that we should pray without ceasing, but how many of us do? I started praying on October 19th, 2012, the day that Beth's doctor thought she might have cancer. I continued to be in an almost constant state of prayer for the next three years.

We were undoubtedly all "prayed up" and feeling confident when we began our early morning drive into downtown Philadelphia on Wednesday, November 14th. We had to drive over an hour to reach the hospital.

After the nurses finished prepping Beth, Kirstyn and I hugged and kissed her before they rolled her away. We then retreated to the waiting area, which looked like a terminal at a major airport. There were computer screens on the walls tracking all the patients that were having surgery that day. The screens informed you when a patient was in surgery, what surgery room they were in, the name of the surgeon and the estimated time of completion. It then posted when the procedure was complete, and when the patient was in recovery.

I tried to read a book while we waited, but I couldn't concentrate on anything except Beth. I decided the best way to spend my time was to pray. I asked the Lord to be with her and to grant the doctors and nurses wisdom as they worked on her. I begged God to help them remove all the cancer.

That afternoon was one of the longest of my life. The hands on the clock never moved more slowly. The wait and uncertainty were excruciating. When fear began to overtake me, I asked God to give me peace.

2

The Call that Changed Everything

I don't remember exactly how long the surgery lasted, but it seemed like an eternity. I'm guessing it took at least five to six hours. Dr. John planned to perform a total hysterectomy, hoping the cancer was confined to Beth's uterus. He seemed confident that he could get it all, but cautioned us that a surgeon never knows for sure what is going on inside of a patient until they open them up.

The hospital was enormous, so big, in fact, that when the doctor completes the surgery, he doesn't come to the waiting area to talk to you in person. You wait for a phone call. When the lady at the desk finally called my name, Kirstyn and I jumped up immediately. When I answered the phone, Dr. John said, "I removed as much as I could. **Unfortunately,** this is a more aggressive form of cancer than I thought, and it has spread throughout her abdomen. I'm afraid our only course of action will be chemotherapy, because it is spread throughout many of her vital organs."

Somewhere around the word "**unfortunately**" it felt like a bomb exploded inside my brain, and I had trouble comprehending anything that he said from that point on. Kirstyn saw that I was dazed, and she grabbed the phone. She immediately went into nursing mode, and started asking questions that only a trained nurse would know to ask like, "How much has it spread? Can you cut any more out? Why can't you radiate?" After she hung up, we found our way into a back room away from the others in the waiting room. We hugged and cried for a long time and then started calling family members around the country. It is difficult to function when you get such devastating news but, somehow, we got the word out to our family and closest friends. We asked them to put Beth's name at the top of every prayer chain.

When the computer screen finally informed us that Beth was out of recovery and on her way to a room, Kirstyn and I hurried to meet her. We were hoping she was still under the influence of the anesthesia, so she wouldn't ask us how the surgery went. As I was putting an extra pillow under her head and kissing her goodnight, she looked at me and said, "Did they get it all?" I responded, "You still have a little bit in your tummy Cakies. So you will need to have some chemo treatments, but you're going be ok." She said, "alright" and then dozed off.

As we drove home from the hospital that night, Kirstyn and I talked about the uphill climb we were facing. We had no idea how difficult the next three years would be. It is probably good that the Lord only gives us one day at a time. If we had known what was ahead, we might not have had the strength to face it.

By the time I dropped Kirstyn off that night and made it home myself, it was after 11 p.m. The nurses had told me that Dr. John likes to visit his patients early in the morning. I was determined to be there when he broke the news to Beth.

3

A Drive Back in Time

I tossed and turned for a few hours that night, and finally decided to get out of bed at 3 a.m. Sleep was out of the question. As I drove in the dark toward downtown Philly early that November morning, my mind flashed back to the day I met Beth thirty-four years earlier. A train ride into Chicago in late September of 1978 changed my life forever.

I began my career in television in 1977 working for ABC affiliate, KMTC-TV, Channel 27 in Springfield, Missouri. That was the year I graduated from Evangel College in Springfield. While visiting the school for homecoming festivities, I heard the TV station was hiring. One of my college communications professors helped me line up an interview with the owner of the station. During the interview, I told him that I was willing to do anything, including sweeping the studio floors. I wanted him to know how badly I wanted that job. A few days later, he called and offered me a job working in the newsroom. I accepted without even asking about the salary.

About a month after I started, the sportscaster for the evening newscast was relieved of his duties. I was asked to audition for the job. I'll never forget the day my boss said they were going to give me a live shot on the news! I was so excited I could hardly contain myself!

My "live audition" went very well, and suddenly, at the age of twenty- three, I was an on-air sportscaster for the ABC affiliate in Springfield, Missouri. I felt on top of the world, and I was making a whopping $2.80 an hour!

I eventually got a raise to $2.85 an hour, which I thought was pretty good at the time, but soon I began to grow restless in the job. There were five colleges in Springfield, so there was an active sports scene to cover. I worked for a small, "low budget" station; the news department only had one mobile camera to cover both the news and sports. As a result, I wasn't able to get out very often to actually cover the sports scene. I became bored reading the teleprompter every night, but I became fascinated with the production people who worked "behind the scenes" to make the newscast happen. I would often stay afterward to talk to the director and the editor about television production. It seemed to me they made magic. I became especially interested in editing.

In the summer of 1978, I received a phone call from a college buddy of mine named Norm Mintle. Norm was a senior at Evangel College when I was a freshman. We lived in the "jock dorm" where the scholarship athletes resided. Norm was a soccer player, and I was on the baseball team. His parents were missionaries in South America, so Norm grew up in regions where *futbol* is king — he practically had a soccer ball attached to his foot from the time he was a kid.

Norm and I became good friends. He dated, and eventually married a girl from my hometown in St. Joe, Michigan, named Linda Marquardt. Linda and I were born in the same hospital just a few days apart. We grew up attending the same church and the same school. Today, she is Dr. Linda Mintle, and is a well known marriage and family therapist, as well as a highly published author and sought after speaker.

Norm was working in Public Relations for a Christian Television station in Chicago called WCFC-TV, Channel 38. He asked if I would be interested in coming to Chicago to see the station, and interview with the Production Manager about a job working on the production crew. I said yes even though I had no production experience.

The studio of Channel 38 was on the 44th floor of the Civic Opera Building located at 20 North Wacker Drive in Chicago. Even though the studio was tiny and the equipment was outdated, I felt the Lord tugging on my heart to move there and work on the production crew. The starting pay was an incredible $5.00 an hour. Of course, I never looked into the cost of living in Chicago, which was substantially higher than in Springfield, Missouri. I started working at Channel 38 in August of 1978. I traded my sportscaster job for a position working "behind the camera."

A friend of mine from Springfield, Brian Roland, took a job as a director at Channel 38 about the same time. We decided to rent an apartment together in the same complex where Norm and Linda were living. Brian had also graduated from Evangel. In fact, he sold me a life insurance policy (that I didn't need and couldn't afford) during my freshman year. In spite of that, Brian and I remain great friends to this day.

One afternoon in late September of 1978, I was riding the Burlington Northern train into Chicago. I worked from 1 p.m. to 10 p.m. every night on the production crew of Channel 38's nightly flagship program. I was trying to read a book about television production when the train stopped in Downer's Grove, Illinois. I noticed an adorable young woman get on the train. Surprisingly, she sat in the seat directly in front of me! Since I didn't get a good look at her face, I kept trying to see her reflection in the window. I don't know what possessed me, but I tapped her on the shoulder and asked if I could come up and sit next to her. She gave me the brightest smile and said, "Sure!" I had no idea that my life was about to change forever.

We talked all the way into the city. When we exited the train at Union Station in Chicago, I asked where she worked. When she said, "The Civic Opera Building on the corner of Wacker and Madison!" I said, "That's the building I work in!" What were the odds?

When we arrived at our building, I asked her if she had time to grab a bite to eat in the cafeteria on the third floor. Again I received a very enthusiastic "Sure!" I figured I might as well keep shooting since I seemed to be on a hot streak. We went through the cafeteria line and got our food. When I went to pay the cashier, I searched my pockets, my wallet and my briefcase for money. Much to my chagrin, I discovered that I did not have a single penny on me! I was so embarrassed to tell her that I didn't have any money, so she would have to pay for our food. I promised I would make it up to her by taking her to lunch later in the week. She laughed and said that would be fine.

I made good on my promise. I took her out two days later to a nice Italian restaurant that I couldn't afford. I figured she was worth it, and I was right. That meal led to thousands of other meals. That girl was Elizabeth Johnson, who would one day become Elizabeth Wheeler. The day we met on the train was September 21st, 1978.

The girl I met on the train.

As I drove on towards Philadelphia in the early morning hours on November 15, 2012, an entire "highlight reel" of our thirty-four years together played in my mind. I thought about the dates we had gone on, our wedding, vacations, the births of our two daughters, graduations, the birth of our grandson and many other beautiful moments we had shared. As these memories flooded my mind, I was overwhelmed with sadness. I felt like I was drowning in grief, to the point where I could barely breathe. I called the only person I knew would be awake at 4 a.m.

Todd Pohlig is the drummer for Blue Sky Band. This is the classic rock band I have played with since 2004. We perform for charitable events to help raise money for various organizations and causes in the greater Philadelphia area. The name Blue Sky comes from a song by the Allman Brothers. The band comprises seven guys from a wide range of professions. We have a physical therapist, a couple of bankers, a neurologist, an engineer, a builder and a former QVC host. Nobody in the band takes a dime for playing at these events, so all of the money raised can go directly to the charity. Todd is a builder, and he had told me that he is usually up and out the door by 4 a.m.

Todd answered his phone immediately. I told him about Beth's surgery. I was an emotional wreck, and I was crying through most of the conversation. I don't remember exactly what he said, but I know that he did what a good friend does in a situation like that. He took time to listen. He empathized with me and offered his prayers, support and help with anything I needed. He has no idea how comforting his voice was to me that morning. A friend in need is surely a friend indeed!

Beth was asleep when I walked into her hospital room, so I sat quietly next to her bed and just stared at her as she slept. And I prayed. I thanked the Lord for letting me spend the last thirty-four years of my life with this woman who was so full of unconditional love and compassion. I begged God to give us more time together so that I could tell her and show her how much I loved her. God answered my prayer.

When she woke up around five- thirty she looked at me and said, "Cakies, what are you doing here so early?" I said something like, "I missed you, and I couldn't sleep, so I came back down." She gave me her signature sweet smile that told me she thought I was a little crazy but that she was happy to see me.

Dr. John came by early and was surprisingly upbeat and positive. He explained to us that Beth had some tumors in her stomach that he couldn't cut out. According to him, the cancer was like a blanket of many small tumors that, unfortunately, covered a lot of her vital organs. Radiation was not an option, but he seemed confident that the chemo would shrink the tumors. His words gave us hope that the chemo could work so while we were still very concerned we both felt like some of the weight had been lifted from our shoulders.

I decided to host my show that night on QVC. Beth and I thought it might be good for me to work. I thought it would help me to get my mind on something else for a while. Since I didn't know what the future held, and how much work I might have to miss, I wanted to host my shows while I still could.

When I walked into QVC Studio Park that night I was feeling much more emotional than I anticipated. I wasn't ready to tell anyone what we were going through except for my boss, Jack Comstock, and my scheduler, Mary Harlyvetch. I didn't want anyone else to know.

The job of a QVC host is challenging. It requires a lot of focus since it is unscripted "live" TV. I didn't want the distraction of people consoling me while I was preparing for a show. While I truly appreciated everyone's concern, and I worked with the best people on the planet, I knew that I was emotionally fragile. I didn't want to have an emotional breakdown on national TV. It is extremely difficult to be a cheerful, upbeat host on live television when you are going through something challenging in your personal life. I developed a technique of going to my mailbox and figuratively putting my problems there. I told myself that I would pick them up after the show.

When you work in front of live television cameras, all of your mistakes happen in front of a lot of people, so I was in "hyper-focus mode" that night. Making it through that show was far more difficult than I imagined it would be. But as they say in the business, "The show must go on!"

We are all expected to be professionals in our chosen occupation day in and day out. During Beth's sickness, however, there were times when I wished I could hide in a cubicle or an office. There is no hiding when you work in front of the cameras. Before my show, I stayed in my dressing room in the host lounge until I absolutely had to come out to meet with the producers and guests. That night was the first of several hundred tough nights for me on air at QVC. Eventually I did tell a lot of my co-workers about Beth's cancer, and everyone was incredibly supportive. I felt very fortunate that QVC is a company that cares about its customers *and* its employees. It was a great blessing for me to be a part of that great company for twenty- nine years.

4

*W*orried About Everyone Else

When I visited Beth two days after her surgery, she introduced me to her new roommate a lovely woman who I'm guessing was in her late seventies. As Beth would always do, she welcomed this woman with open arms and made her feel instantly at home.

By the time I arrived, Beth knew the names of her children and grandchildren, and she had shared pictures and stories of ours. My Cakies never wanted anybody to feel left out or alone, so she included this lady in our conversation all day long until her daughter came to visit that evening. This was Beth at her best. She treated this lady like she was her best friend.

Kirstyn called Beth the morning that she was to be released from the hospital. She asked, "Mom, are you excited to come home today?" There was a hesitation in Beth's voice. Kirstyn asked again, "Mom, are you excited to come home?"

Beth responded that she was, but she was also very concerned about her roommate. She thought this lady needed more attention than the nurses were giving her. Apparently, Beth had been playing the roles of both patient recovering from major surgery *and* nurse to her roommate. She told me she often got up at night to get this lady a cold washcloth when she was too warm. She said that she even helped her to the bathroom if the nurses didn't respond promptly. This is who Beth was. She always worried about everyone else, no matter what she was going through herself.

Her genuine love and concern for others were evident to all who came in contact with her. When we were in our late twenties, we attended the wedding of one of Beth's high school friends. We were sitting at a table with several of our friends at the reception. Everyone at our table was laughing and having a great time, but Beth noticed an elderly gentleman sitting all alone. Nobody was paying any attention to him. This bothered her, so she asked everyone at our table if we would mind if she invited him to join us. We all told her that would be fine. The next thing we knew, Beth was helping this man up from his seat and walking him over to our table. She pulled up a chair for him right next to hers and introduced him to everyone.

This man ended up having a wonderful time that day. You could see the excitement and appreciation on his face. Beth made him so happy! She not only brought him to the table, but she also made him feel like he was the most important person in the world! I knew that night that she was the girl I wanted to marry. Fortunately, when I finally asked her a few years later, she said, "Yes!"

One of Beth's best friends at this time was Fran Mardjetko. They were inseparable. Every morning they rode the same train together because they both worked in downtown Chicago. One day they were very late for their train so they were running as fast as they could go, in high heels, to jump on the train before it left the station. As they were running, Fran dropped her makeup case, and her makeup spilled all over the ground. Beth stopped to pick it all up.

Fran yelled back to her to forget about it and get on the train. But Beth was more concerned about Fran's makeup because she didn't want her friend to have to buy more. Fran hopped on the train and yelled for the conductor to wait for her best friend, but just as Beth was about to jump on, the doors closed in her face, and the train started pulling away. Fran pounded on the doors and shouted to the conductor to stop the train. "Don't leave my best friend!" she cried. It was too late. Beth just waved as the train pulled away from the station.

Fran cried for several minutes as she realized that Beth was going to be late for work because she stopped to pick up her makeup. Beth had to wait another half hour for the next train into the city. She ended up being late for work that day, but she did save all of Fran's makeup. That is the kind of friend Beth was.

It was during this time in our relationship that we began taking weekend trips to South Haven, Michigan to visit my dad and his wife, Sally. Beth knew that I wanted to spend some time alone with my dad. I hadn't been able to do that since I was a young boy. After he and my mom divorced when I was eleven years old, I never had a chance to be alone with him. Whenever I saw him, he was with his second wife and a couple of her children, or he was working on patients at his dental practice where I often visited him. I longed to spend some one- on- one time with him.

Sally was my dad's third wife. Their home was on the shore of Lake Michigan. One day Beth, my dad and I went for a walk on the beach. When we were about a half-mile down the beach, Beth announced that she had to run back to the house to use the bathroom. She said, "See you later!" and took off running. She did this so that I could have time alone with my dad—it was her way of granting my wish.

It was a little awkward when she first left us, but soon the conversation flowed. I think my dad realized that day that I wasn't going to judge him or make him feel sorry for the divorce.

We didn't return to the house until well after sunset that evening. My dad and I spent over three hours that day just walking and talking. I believe we "rediscovered" each other. It was the start of a new relationship with my dad. Every time we visited from that day on, he wanted to carve out time for just the two of us. We became friends and remained close until the day he died in May of 1996. I owe it all to Beth. She is the one who made it happen.

My dad adored Beth, and so did my dad's dad, Grandpa Joe Wheeler. When Grandma Wheeler died, he was devastated. They had been married for over sixty years. Beth and I drove from Chicago to South Haven, Michigan to attend her funeral.

When we walked into Grandpa's house, we found him sitting in his favorite chair. He was crying, and he looked lost. Beth walked right up to him and threw her arms around him. She hugged him for a long time and kept telling him how sorry she was.

When we went to the church for Grandma's funeral, he wanted Beth to sit next to him. When our family went to a restaurant after the service he, again, wanted her next to him. She held his hand all day long and comforted him as only she could. Keep in mind that Beth and I were just dating at the time. She wasn't even related to my grandfather. His two daughters and two sons and their wives and children were there. But Beth was the one he wanted next to him the entire weekend.

A few months later, I went to South Haven to see my dad. For some reason, Beth didn't come with me. When my dad and I walked into grandpa's house, he asked me where she was. When I told him she didn't come with me, he said if I didn't bring her on my next visit he wasn't going to let me in his house!

Finally, one of the few times I had to miss Beth's chemo treatment she met a new nurse. She called me on her way home to tell me all about her. She was very impressed with her kindness and her desire to help others. Beth told me this woman spent her Sunday afternoons in the winter helping people who lived on the street find warm shelter. She got involved with this initiative through her church.

At one point, the woman noticed Beth's Ugg boots and complimented her on them. Beth told her they were so warm and comfy that she wore them everywhere she went in the winter. She then told this nurse that she should buy herself a pair to wear when she worked with the street people. She told Beth that she would love a pair but that she couldn't afford to buy them because her husband wasn't able to work due to a physical disability. I knew what was coming next. Beth asked, "Oh Cakies, can we please buy her a pair of Ugg boots?" I said, "Of course we can! But do you know her size?" She did. She had asked the lady and had written it down.

We gave this nurse her own pair of Ugg boots at our very next chemo session and she just went to pieces. She thanked us for them so many times that you would have thought we had bought her a house. I know that buying this nurse those boots brought Beth an amazing amount of joy. She was always teaching me that it is so much better (and more fun) to give than to receive.

5

Time to Grow Up!

I had a fear of marriage when I started dating Beth. Perhaps it had something to do with the fact that my parents were divorced when I was eleven years old. I didn't spend much time with my dad after the divorce. I usually had to ride my bike (with the banana seat and the high handle bars) to his dental practice, which was seven blocks from my house. I tried to talk to him while he worked on his patients. During these visits, he would eventually say, "Hey Danny! Here's a couple of bucks go buy yourself some baseball cards!" I then rode off on my bike to the drugstore to buy baseball cards. Finally one day I said to him, "Dad I don't want your money, and I don't need any more baseball cards. I just want to spend time with you!"

Perhaps I was also afraid that I would never make enough money to support a wife and children. When Beth and I met in 1978, I was barely making enough to pay my bills. I remember never having any extra money left over after paying the rent, my monthly train ticket into Chicago, gas for my car and groceries. Brian Roland and I shared an apartment in Lisle, Illinois, that was probably beyond our financial means at the time. I remember that first year our monthly rent was $380. My half was a whopping $190! That seemed like an exorbitant amount of money at the time.

I rarely had enough money to take Beth out for a date. Once in a while, however, we would go to a movie at the Tivoli Theatre in Downer's Grove, Illinois. They didn't show first-run movies, but the tickets were only a dollar apiece! We thoroughly enjoyed seeing movies there, and we could even afford to split a box of popcorn because it was just fifty cents!

One of my childhood friends, Joel Kruggel, was the pastor of a church in Bolingbrook, Illinois located only about fifteen minutes from my apartment in Lisle. Beth and I became involved with his church. Because I played guitar, Joel asked me to lead the singing for the Sunday morning services. I also taught the adult Sunday school class. It was exciting to watch our little church grow. We didn't own a church building, so we began meeting in a classroom at the local middle school. We later graduated to the band room and finally the cafeteria. It was so much fun to work with Joel and his wife, Victoria, who also grew up in my hometown.

The four of us enjoyed going to roller skate after church on Sunday afternoons. There was a huge roller skating rink nearby. Beth and I loved dancing together so skating felt like we were dancing on wheels.

Victoria's mom, Betty, had been my very first boss when I started working as a teenager. She owned a fast food restaurant in my hometown of St. Joe, Michigan called the Chicken Coop. I fried chicken and waited on customers there when I was in high school. I got my first taste of selling working there. The buckets that we put the chicken in had a saying along the top that read, "Only one life, 'twill soon be past, only what's done for Christ will last." I never forgot that saying or the delicious taste of the chicken. To this day when I go back to my hometown, my first stop is the Chicken Coop.

After Beth and I had been dating for six and a half years,

I think she was tired of waiting for me to put a ring on her finger: she started dating another guy to make me jealous. He was crazy about her and was asking her out all the time, so I decided I better pop the question. One night I called her up and told her to meet me at the train station—because we had met on the train. When she showed up, I made a Bogart-like entrance wearing a trench coat. I pulled out a game of *Parcheesi* with her engagement ring inside. Because of my grandparents' love for the game, Beth and I had always wanted to grow old together and play *Parcheesi*. As soon as she saw the *Parcheesi* box, she knew I was going to ask her to marry me.

We were both thirty years old when we married. Our wedding was a modest ceremony in Quincy, Illinois. My brother-in-law, Reverend Ronn Read, was the pastor of Lighthouse Baptist Church. Ronn, my sister Mary Jane and their young family, had been living in Quincy for a few years at the time. Since my mom also lived there, we decided to have the wedding in Quincy.

I had two thousand dollars in my savings account at the time, and we spent every penny of it on the wedding. Beth's dad had passed away long before—when she was only fourteen years old. He succumbed to a rare blood disease at just 46 years of age. Her mom was living on a modest salary, so we decided to do a wedding on my meager savings. Beth shopped around and found a beautiful wedding dress for just $175. We got the church for free, since Ronn was the pastor, and we held the reception in the basement. Because we were on such a limited budget, we only invited family and a few close friends. We exchanged our vows on December 22, 1984, at the Lighthouse Baptist Church in Quincy, Illinois in front of about thirty-five people. It was the best day and the best decision of my life.

Beth and I stayed at the Quincy Holiday Inn on our wedding night. Our moms wanted to come up and see our room after the wedding. We were happy to show it to them, but an hour later they were still there. It seemed like an eternity, and we were wondering if they were ever going to leave! After all, it was our wedding night! They finally made their exit, after we dropped numerous hints!

We waited until April of '85 to go on our honeymoon because we were both working full- time and had used all our vacation time for 1984. As a wedding gift, a good friend of mine, Jim Sauter, gave us a week at his family's condo at a high- end resort in West Palm Beach. We were thrilled to stay at such a beautiful place. The only thing we could afford on our own back then would have been a tent at a campground. About a year later, we actually moved in with Jim and another guy named Ken Nelson. Jim purchased an amazing home in Naperville, Illinois and he had plenty of room and asked us to move in. The rent was very affordable and we were blessed to live in a gorgeous four- bedroom home for about a year and a half. We had a very private, very spacious bedroom upstairs and our own private bathroom. Kirstyn had her own nursery right next to our room. Jim and Ken were great roommates. I'm sure the neighbors wondered what was happening to their neighborhood when three guys and a pregnant woman moved into that beautiful home. Kirstyn spent the first year of her life living there with her parents and our two good friends.

We didn't fit the profile of the typical residents at this particular resort in West Palm Beach. We weren't allowed to use the tennis courts on the grounds because neither one of us owned an all-white tennis outfit! Instead, we drove about three blocks away and played on the public courts. We laughed about that for the next thirty-one years!

Beth and I always enjoyed the simple things in life, but staying at this beautiful place was a real treat. We tried our best to blend in and act like we belonged. For one week we got a taste of how the rich and the famous live.

We drove up to Orlando to spend a day at Disney World

with a couple of high school buddies of mine named Mike Hanners and John Cooke. That was a great memory for us. It was the first time either of us had been there. We had no idea at the time that we would be back twenty-eight years later for our final visit there together.

6

$\mathcal{S}$tage 4

After Beth's initial surgery, we scheduled a follow-up visit with Dr. John for Tuesday, December 11th, 2012. His office was in a vast medical complex across the street from the hospital where he performed Beth's surgery. Kirstyn, Beth and I were escorted into his office. Just before he walked in, I noticed Beth's report was lying on his desk. Directly below her name, I read the words "Stage 4 Cancer." I tried to get Beth's attention away from the desk because I didn't want her to see it. I texted Kirstyn who was sitting on the other side of Beth, and I told her what it said. Her response was, "Oh No!"

When Dr. John came in he was once again very upbeat and positive. He told us that he wanted Beth to begin chemotherapy the first week in January of 2013. He said he wanted to use two drugs that had a good record of success in the treatment of cancer. Since her cancer started in the lining of her uterus, it was called endometrial cancer. He explained that Beth might be nauseous for a day or two after the treatment, but he told us he would prescribe a drug to help with that. We walked out of his office with several prescriptions that day. They were the first of many more to come.

He didn't tell us that Beth's cancer was stage 4 during that visit. But I will never forget how I felt when I saw Beth's report on his desk. I was devastated.

At the end of our meeting, Dr. John recommended that we take a nice vacation before we began the chemo treatments. He advised us to go somewhere special, somewhere we had always wanted to go.

On the ride home, Beth expressed concern over the fact that he told us to take a "special" vacation. She thought that meant that she didn't have long to live. I said I thought the reason was that she would probably not feel like traveling anywhere once we began the chemo treatments. I was doing my best to keep a positive attitude.

By the time we got home, Beth had decided that she wanted to go back to Disney World. She thought it would be fun to take our grandson, Cole, who was three- years- old at the time. I agreed that we would probably feel better seeing the Magic Kingdom through his eyes.

I contacted my travel agent the very next day and told him to book "the vacation of a lifetime" to Disney World. My instructions were to spare no expense. Kirstyn, Jeff, Cole, Kelsey, Beth and I flew first class both ways. We had two rooms reserved at the Polynesian Resort located directly across the lake from the Magic Kingdom. We had unlimited passes to all of the attractions. We dined at some of the best restaurants on the grounds. I wanted this trip to be memorable, and for the first time in my life, I didn't care what it cost.

When we arrived at the airline ticket counter at the Philadelphia airport to check in on December 26, 2012, the lady behind the counter recognized me from QVC. She told me that she was a big fan and enjoyed watching me. I appreciated the attention and enjoyed talking to her, but I was also hoping she was paying attention to what she was doing. After she put all of our bags on the conveyor belt, she noticed that she was holding an extra tag to Orlando. I said, "I hope you didn't mislabel one of our bags and send it to the wrong city. Could you please go back and look for our bags to make sure they are all tagged for Orlando?"

She was gone for what seemed like an hour, but was probably fifteen minutes. When she came back, she apologized because she couldn't find our bags. We had to hope they would all make it to Orlando. As much as I love talking with fans, I felt like she had not done her job, and it bothered me. My prayer was: if she had mislabeled one of our bags, that it would be mine and not Beth's. She had several prescription drugs that she needed for pain, and I wanted her to enjoy every minute of our trip. When we landed in Orlando, all of our bags showed up except for Beth's.

After we checked into the Polynesian, Beth and I went directly to the gift shop to look for some comfy clothes for her to wear until her suitcase arrived. We then went to the local drug store to get her some pain meds. She made it through the night and, fortunately, her suitcase arrived the next afternoon from West Palm Beach. The lady from the airlines, who made the mistake, wrote me a very apologetic message on my QVC Facebook page. I didn't see it until after we returned home. I wrote her back and told her not to worry about it. Everything had worked out, and mistakes do happen.

In spite of the suitcase mishap, we had a fantastic time in Orlando. Beth felt well, and we saw as much of Disney World as we could. While our kids liked the more exhilarating rides, Beth and I enjoyed the more mild attractions like The Hall of Presidents, Carousel of Progress and the Haunted Mansion. I always loved the fast, wild rides as a kid, but now that I'm older, I definitely prefer the more mellow ones.

It was a magical trip to a magical place. Cole loved the parade at the end of each evening. Beth thoroughly enjoyed the Magic Kingdom Castle Light Show. It was spectacular! I remember watching her face light up as she watched that show.

I wanted to freeze time. I wanted the moment to last forever. As hard as we all tried to forget about Beth's cancer for a few days, it was always there in the back of our minds. Beth didn't talk about it much at this time. She told me she wanted to forget about it and "live in the moment."

Everything changes immediately when you or a loved one receives a diagnosis of cancer. As I mentioned earlier, our priorities turned upside down but ultimately right side up in an instant. I must have told Beth that I loved her seven to eight times a day every day after we learned about her cancer. I will never regret it. Life is short whether you live to be ten, sixty-one or ninety- nine. Each day is a precious gift. We can't be wasting our time worrying about things that don't matter in the long run. Beth always said, "Don't sweat the small stuff." After her diagnosis, our other problems no longer seemed like problems.

When you go through a major crisis, it is hard to listen to other people complaining about little things like the weather or having to work an extra hour. Stage 4 cancer pretty much dwarfs the other stuff we go through. When I overheard people complaining about these little "problems" I had to bite my lip. I always wanted to interrupt and tell them "you have no idea what real problems are. Let me tell you about a real problem!"

Be thankful every day for your health, your family and your friends. Count your blessings and try to put each day's problems into perspective. If you and your family are healthy be thankful. If you or a loved one is facing a health issue, pour your time and your love into the situation. Remember that things are never quite as bad as they seem and no matter what the problem is that you are facing don't forget this saying: "This too shall pass."

7

Chemo "Dates"

None of us were excited about returning home from our vacation. We knew Beth was facing her first chemotherapy treatment on January 3, 2013. When we crawled into bed the night before, Beth told me she was afraid of what the chemo was going to do to her. She had read that most patients experienced a great deal of nausea and achiness afterward. I felt her fear and wished I could do the treatment for her.

I had to work the day of her first treatment, so Kirstyn went with her. Kirstyn always managed to keep her mom laughing through treatments and procedures. I was glad she could be with her for the first one. That was one of only three chemo treatments that I missed during the next three years. She came through the first one feeling ok, but she was exhausted by the time she got home. The medical facility is a minimum of an hour drive from our home. If we got caught in rush hour traffic, it took up to two hours each way.

Our typical chemo day began at 6 a.m. We had to be on the road by 6:45 a.m. to beat the traffic. We usually waited for a half-hour to see the doctor then we spent another half-hour with the doctor. Then we waited another fifteen to twenty minutes to get assigned to a chemo suite. Once in the suite, the nurse checked all of Beth's vital signs and then gave her a bag of fluids before each drug. The fluids took a half-hour, and the drugs took one to two hours each. All in all, it usually took about six hours for each session. When you add the commute time both ways, it was an all-day affair.

The first two chemo drugs they used knocked Beth out of commission for two to three days afterward. She experienced severe nausea and fatigue and spent many hours curled up in pain on the bathroom floor. I'm sure the anti-nausea medication helped, so I can't imagine how hard it would have been for her without it.

We had a large plastic bag filled with all of Beth's bottles of prescription drugs at the time. She had pills for nausea, pain, nerves, etc. So along with the chemo drugs, she had to take drugs to help with the side effects. I had to make a spreadsheet to tell us what each medication was for, the dosage and frequency of use.

Cancer and chemo are extremely taxing on the immune system, so we had to make sure that Beth was never around anyone who was sick. We were always concerned about the possibility of infection.

Cakies and I decided early on in her treatment that we would try to make her chemo days fun, so we pretended the treatment days were "dates." When we first arrived at the medical building, I went straight to the bakery on the first floor. I bought two chocolate croissants while she went upstairs and checked in for her doctor's appointment.

In the early years of our dating life, we liked to stop at a French bakery in Chicago on our way to work in the morning. We always ordered two chocolate croissants. When we discovered the bakery on the first floor of this medical building made chocolate croissants, we were excited. They reminded us of a happier time.

When we finally checked into a chemo suite, I warmed the

croissants up in a microwave, and we enjoyed them together before her treatment began. I returned to the same bakery around noon to order two bowls of their delicious Tomato Basil soup. As I write this, I realize how much I miss those days. Even though the treatments were physically hard on Beth, at least we were together. I think we managed to make the best of the situation.

Beth's strength and courage amazed me every single day. She kept a positive attitude and told me that she was thankful for the chemotherapy because it was keeping her alive. Everyone who worked on the gynecological oncology wing of this medical building fell in love with Beth. From the receptionists to the nurses and the physician's assistants to the doctors, everyone knew Beth Wheeler, and they smiled when they saw her. We often took a box of Cheryl's cookies for all of the workers. These were amazingly delicious cookies that we offered on QVC. The medical personnel loved them so much that every time we walked in, someone invariably asked if we brought the cookies.

Beth made friends, not only with the staff, but with the other patients as well. There was a lady named Margie who recognized me from QVC. She said she was a big fan and she instantly fell in love with Beth, like everyone else. We always looked forward to seeing her. She had an infectious personality and positive attitude. And she always had snacks to share. Margie's husband, Steve, was quiet and somewhat introverted. Whenever he thought Margie was talking too much, he would tell her that it was "time to leave these poor people alone." Beth and I never minded talking with Margie. We were always happy to see them.

Margie and Steve stopped showing up for chemo—we missed seeing them for several weeks and finally thought to ask about them...the nurse told us that Margie had passed away. It hit us hard—and reminded us that every day was a gift, and that we were in a life and death battle.

A few months into her chemotherapy, Beth's hair began falling out in clumps. This was very hard for her. A woman's hair is her crown, and even though she knew this was going to happen, I could see the sadness and concern on her face. One day she called me at work and said, "I did it. I cut it all off!" She told me she drove past the hair salon several times trying to work up the courage to have her hair buzzed off. Once she did it, she said that she felt "empowered."

As summer approached, we began looking forward to our vacation in Stone Harbor, New Jersey. We rented a beach house that was located just a half block from the ocean. Between our family and Jeff's family (Kirstyn's husband) we had fourteen people staying for a week in a six- bedroom house.

The Thursday before our vacation was to begin, Beth called me at QVC. I immediately knew something was wrong. "Cakies, it didn't work. The chemo didn't work," she said.

I asked, "What do you mean it didn't work?"

She said, "I am reading my report on the website, and all of my tumors grew." I'll never forget the disappointment in her voice. It was devastating for me to watch her go through almost six months of arduous chemo treatments and lose all her hair only to find out the tumors grew. They were going to have to try a different combination of chemo drugs.

We prayed together that night and asked the Lord to give the doctors wisdom regarding the next step in her treatment. We then decided we were going to try to enjoy our vacation at the beach and worry about the future when we came back. This was easier said than done.

I woke up early that first morning at the beach. I walked into the kitchen where Kirstyn's in-laws, Ed and Nancy Hauser, were already drinking their coffee. As I poured myself a cup, I broke down and started crying uncontrollably. I told them that the chemo didn't work, and I admitted that I was scared. They were kind and understanding, and they consoled me. Somehow I managed to pull myself together before Beth woke up.

Kirstyn was expecting her second child at the time—and wanted all of us to learn the gender of the baby while the family was together. She'd had a scan the week before and told the doctor to put the results in an envelope and not tell her. Kirstyn then gave the envelope to one of her best friends and instructed her to buy either a boy or girl teddy bear based on the results, wrap it up and send it along with Kirstyn to the shore.

The first night after everyone had arrived at the beach, the entire family gathered in the spacious living room of our beach house. Kirstyn gave the wrapped box to our grandson, Cole, and told him to open it to see if the baby was going to be a boy or girl. Her friend, Becky, had wrapped several boxes and put one inside the other. It took little Cole a long time to open all the boxes. Sighs and laughter met each new package. When he finally unwrapped the last box, there was a Boy bear inside!

I recorded video of the entire event. You can hear Beth's infectious laugh throughout the video. My niece, Terra, once said that Hollywood should have used her aunt Beth's laugh for a laugh track. When Beth Wheeler laughed, it filled the room and made everyone in it feel joyful. She didn't hold anything back. She truly knew how to enjoy the funny side of life.

That was the highlight of our 2013 summer vacation. We managed to have a good time the rest of the week. It was reassuring to see Beth laughing and enjoying the hot, sunny days on the beach and the warm summer evenings on the deck. After returning from the beach every day, we all gathered and formed what we called, "The Circle of Love" to enjoy appetizers and drinks together before dinner.

The week at the beach was a much-needed oasis in our cancer battle. While everyone had an enjoyable time, the fact that Beth had Stage 4 Cancer was always in the back of our minds. I remember glancing at Beth when she wasn't looking and just feeling so thankful that she was with us. I wanted to savor every minute we had together. I wish I'd had that attitude during our entire marriage. There were times when I lost sight of what was important. I think a lot of us tell ourselves that someday things will slow down and we'll have more time to be with our families and loved ones. Before we know it, we're sixty years old, and we're still racing around trying to keep up with life instead of really living it. When the doctor told us Beth had cancer, I decided it was time to stop rushing.

One night at the beach, as we all sat down for dinner, Nancy, Kirstyn's mother-in-law, suggested we go around the table and say something nice about the person seated to our right. I was on Kirstyn's right, and when it was her turn, she said that she was proud of the way I was taking care of her mom. She said that she had wondered if I would be able to do it, but she was happy to see that I was coming through with flying colors. Her comment meant a lot to me. I'm pretty sure I cried.

My message to everyone now is to slow down! Smell the roses and spend time with the ones you love. You never know when it will be the last time you are with them. Make the best out of every situation and if you are facing a health crisis with someone in your family face it together! It will make your love stronger!

8

*N*ew Drugs, New Hope

The first combination of chemo drugs had failed to shrink Beth's tumors in six months of treatment, so it was time to try new drugs. Her treatments were stepped up from once every three weeks to every other week.

The side effects of the new drugs were more severe than previously. Nausea and vomiting knocked her out of commission for 3 days after each treatment. She spent hours in the bathroom. Whenever I heard her vomiting, I went in and asked if I could help her in any way. She thanked me but then said that she just wanted to be left alone. I noticed that she was starting to lose her appetite, and when I asked her about it she said that food had a metal taste. She attributed that to the drugs.

After a few rough days, she always rallied. When she finally felt completely better, it was almost time for the next treatment, and the cycle started all over again.

Beth had a powerful will to live. I remember she told me that as bad as the treatments made her feel, it was better than the alternative. She often said that she was just glad to be alive. I don't know how she managed to go through this for the remainder of that year. We were hoping against hope that we would get a good report by Christmas. That would have been the best present ever.

Kirstyn's pregnancy progressed nicely, and on Thursday, October 24, 2013, we welcomed a new addition to our family, Gavin Tayler. Fortunately, he was born in a week when Beth was not scheduled for a chemo treatment, so she felt relatively good. I'll never forget watching her hold baby Gavin in her arms in the hospital. I remember praying that she would be able to watch him grow up.

Our family circled close for the holidays. We never enjoyed Thanksgiving and Christmas more. We tried to savor every moment. We were all keenly aware that every minute, every day and every week is a precious gift not to be taken for granted.

We flew my mom out from Milwaukee for Christmas. At ninety-one years of age, she was beginning to exhibit signs of dementia. I took her to our local mall about a week before the big day. (Yes, I am one of those weird people that actually enjoys going to the mall around Christmas time.) It wouldn't be Christmas for me if I didn't do some last minute shopping in a crowded mall. I think it adds to the excitement of the season.

At one point, my mom and I were in a women's clothing store, and she said she wanted to try on a few items she had found. I told her I was going to go to a nearby toy store to pick up a couple of presents for Cole and Gavin and that I would be right back. I gave her very clear instructions not to leave the store until I returned. About fifteen minutes later, I walked into the store, and she was nowhere to be found! After a couple of trips around the store, I began to panic. I asked everyone I ran into if they had seen her. Nobody had. I started wondering how I would explain to my sisters that I lost mom in a shopping mall!

After about fifteen minutes of searching, I found her standing in front of another store across the aisle. When I asked her why she had left the store, she insisted that she hadn't. She said that she was standing right where I told her. I decided not to argue.

I was just happy I found her. When I called Beth and told her what had happened, she had a good laugh.

Beth had an abdominal scan just before Christmas. The report gave us hope. Some of her tumors were no larger at all from the previous scan, and the others grew only slightly. We thought maybe we had found the right combination of drugs. That was the best Christmas gift we ever received. We decided to celebrate Christmas in a more meaningful way that year. We focused more on the birth of Jesus and on family time than on buying gifts. It was far more significant.

Beth's doctor decided to give her a three-week break from chemo, so she was able to enjoy the holidays free from fatigue and nausea. It was a very merry Christmas indeed!

L to R: Kirstyn, Beth, Kelsey, Me-December 2012.

9

*B*eth's Big Surprise

Our younger daughter Kelsey had signed up for the study abroad program for the spring semester of her junior year at Messiah College. The country she chose for her studies was Thailand. When she told Beth and me about it, we thought it was a nice idea, but neither of us thought she would actually follow through with it.

Kelsey was very shy growing up. As a child, she rarely made eye contact with anyone outside of our family. She still had trouble ordering her own food in a restaurant when she was fourteen. She struggled in elementary school. We had her tested at a local college and discovered she had short-term memory loss which made it very difficult for her to take tests. Through hard work and determination, however, she overcame it all and blossomed into an exceptional student. I'll talk about this more in a later chapter.

Kelsey had never been out of the country, and the idea of her going to the other side of the world for an entire semester seemed impossible. In spite of this, she left for Thailand out of the Baltimore airport a few days after Christmas.

The two long flights overseas were almost unbearable for her. She developed stomach problems on her flight from the U.S.

to South Korea. Her physical ailments continued on the plane to Thailand and for several days after she landed. Things were not going well.

I was attending the Consumer Electronics Show in Las Vegas for QVC that week, but I stayed in constant communication with Kelsey via WhatsApp which is an app you can download to your phone that allows you to text messages overseas. After three days, she told me she couldn't handle it, and she begged me to fly her back home. I said she needed to give it at least two weeks. I reminded her that this was an opportunity of a lifetime and that if she came home so quickly, she might regret it for the rest of her life. Because of the time difference, I was usually up texting her in the middle of the night Vegas time.

Although it was extremely difficult for her, she agreed to give it two weeks. Slowly but surely things began to turn around for her. One night I received a text from her telling me her friend, Kayty, prayed with her and that she was starting to feel better about her situation. She began going to her classes to learn the Thai language and began interacting with the other American students. She also started volunteering at a woman's shelter.

After the first week, all of Kelsey's fears and insecurities melted away, and she started to embrace the experience. She ended up falling in love with the Thai people and their country. By the time she returned home in April, she had many wonderful stories to share about her amazing trip. It truly changed her life and deepened her faith. Today, several years later, she still talks about her desire to return to Thailand.

When I woke up on January 1st, 2014, I realized that Beth's sixtieth birthday was quickly approaching. From our earliest days together, Beth always found a way to get ahold of my calendar and write her birthday in big, bold letters on February 3rd. Every year she reminded her friends and family members that her birthday was coming on that date. I knew I had to pull off something big, and I knew I was going to need help because it was almost impossible to surprise Beth.

I learned about the five W's and the H in my first journalism class in college. These are the questions a good journalist must ask and answer about every story. The five W's are Who, What, When, Where and Why? The H is for How? I figured these applied to planning a party as well as writing a story.

We began with the **Where.** Where could we throw this party? Should we go to Beth's favorite restaurant? Should we rent a banquet hall? Both seemed too impersonal. Kirstyn suggested we ask our neighbor, Dana Poirier, if we could have it at her house. I loved the idea!

Dana and her husband Steve are the "salt of the earth." They own a successful medical supplies company, but they are "down to earth," friendly people. Steve is one of the funniest guys I have ever met. When he tells a story, people are usually laughing so hard, they can barely breathe. Dana and Steve are both wonderful Christian people who love the Lord and love giving to others. Dana was one of Beth's very best friends. The Poiriers own a beautiful home at the end of our street, and they enjoy throwing parties through out the year.

Kirstyn and I quickly decided that their home would be the perfect place to throw the perfect surprise birthday party. We could act like they were having a "Chase Away the Winter Blues" party. Beth wouldn't suspect anything since they were always throwing parties. When I asked Dana if we could use their house, I didn't even have the whole question out before she emphatically said, "YES! Let's do it HERE!"

A surprise sixtieth birthday party for Beth was the **What. When** was critical. If we threw it on Beth's actual birthday, she would figure it out. We decided to go with Friday, January 31st the weekend of the big football game. Beth's favorite NFL team, the Denver Broncos, was playing in the Big Game that year. Her brother, Roy, was also a big Bronco's fan and I was hoping to bring him in for the weekend. I thought it would be nice if they could watch the game together.

Next, we had to answer **Who** as in who would we invite? We came up with a list of about sixty of her closest friends. We then decided we would give her what she would want more than anything else: her family. I decided to fly her mom, brother, and sister-in-law from Chicago and her sister from California.

The toughest of all the questions was **How?** How would we plan it and not get caught? How would we prepare all of the food and not be a burden on the Poiriers? This would be tough because Beth would have her antenna up. How would we get all the guests there before Beth arrived and surprise her?

We pulled it off with many secret phone calls between Kirstyn, Dana and me. We decided the most convenient thing to do regarding food was to have the food delivered by a caterer with warming trays, serving spoons and dinnerware. I made a few visits to a place in West Chester, Pennsylvania called Carlino's. They are renowned for their delicious Italian food and excellent catering. They helped me put together a great menu. A close friend of mine, Anthony Corrado, is a professional chef. He generously offered to arrive a couple of hours early to help the caterers set up and to prepare some extra *hors d'oeuvres* to complete the spread.

The plans were in motion. Beth seemed oblivious to any possibility of a party. In fact, we were watching television the week before, and an ad came on for the super big football game. She commented that it would be so great if Roy could come out for her birthday so they could watch it together. (Little did she know that she would be doing just that!) I acted like I was upset with myself and said, "Oh Cakies, I am the worst husband ever! I have been so busy with work that I didn't have time to plan anything for your birthday. I am so sorry." She responded in her usual, sweet way saying, "It's okay Cakies. We can just have a nice, quiet celebration at home with our family." I remember thinking how surprised she was going to be and I started to get excited about the big party we were about to pull off.

All of the guests were told to arrive at the Poirier's no later than 6:30 p.m. on Friday. About sixty people showed up on time, but I was having a difficult time getting Beth to move. I kept trying to hurry her but, per Murphy's Law, she was moving slower than ever! I told her that I wanted to get down to the party early because I had to work the next day, and I didn't want to stay out late. She told me to relax and that we would leave right after she emptied the dishwasher. By this time it was getting close to seven o'clock. The plan was for me to have her to the Poirier's house by six forty-five! I started helping her empty the dishwasher. She must have wondered why I was putting away the dishes as fast as I could.

Kirstyn called me at seven, so I stepped outside to take her call. She asked me where we were and why it was taking so long. I told her that her mom was moving like a turtle even though I was trying to hurry her along. Kirstyn then had a brilliant idea. She knew her mom would do anything for her grandkids, so she decided to call her and tell her that Gavin had an accident, and she needed diapers and a change of clothes right away. It worked like a charm! Beth immediately got the clothes and the diapers, and we were out the door!

My heart was almost beating out of my chest as we walked up the Poirier's walkway to the front door. I knew what was coming, but Beth had no idea. When we walked in, we were greeted by a very loud "Surprise!!!!!!" People were holding "Happy Birthday Beth!" signs and birthday balloons covered the house. I'll never forget the look on her face as she put her hand over her mouth and looked around in disbelief. She then looked at me and said, "I can't believe you fooled me!" She started crying and then gave me a big hug and a kiss.

When you think back over your life, certain moments stand out as truly unforgettable. This was one of those moments. I wanted to freeze time. Thank God that cell phones can shoot video. I captured the moment on my phone, and I play it back whenever I need to smile.

Beth immediately began walking around the room greeting and hugging everyone. She thanked each person for being there. In the meantime, I was watching my phone for a message because we were waiting for her family to arrive from the airport. We scheduled their flights so they would all land at the Philadelphia airport around the same time. Once they all met, they picked up their rental car and drove straight to the party. Their timing was perfect! They arrived just as Beth finished making her way around the room.

As I slipped outside to bring them in, Kirstyn asked for everyone's attention. She thanked them all for being there and said that we were now going to give Beth what she most wanted for her birthday. I then walked through the door with her family! Beth lost it all over again. She started crying and laughing at the same time as she hugged her mom, her brother, and sister-in-law and finally her sister. I saw pure joy in her eyes as she glanced my way. Kirstyn and I high- fived each other and took a moment to celebrate that we had pulled off the biggest surprise of Beth's life.

It was an unforgettable night. I only wish Kelsey could have been home to celebrate with us, but it would have been way too disruptive to bring her home from Thailand. Other than that, it was perfect.

We have talked about this surprise party several times over the past few years. We always say how happy we are that we did it. It was worth every bit of the time and effort. **(Is there a party that you need to throw for someone you love? Do it! You will never regret it if you do, but you might if you don't!)**

10

$\mathcal{S}$ea Hunt to Nashville

I was so thankful that Beth felt good on her sixtieth birthday weekend. Her family stayed for several days after the party, and she got to watch the Big Game with her brother. Unfortunately, her Denver Broncos lost by a significant margin, but she still enjoyed watching it with Roy.

A few weeks later, Beth's primary specialist, Dr. John, announced that he was leaving the hospital and healthcare system that we were in—he was taking a similar position at another well- known cancer treatment center in the area. He informed us personally that he was leaving but said he would be honored to continue caring for Beth at his new location. We weren't sure if we should follow him or stay where we were to meet his replacement.

We had become good friends with one of his physician assistants whom I'll refer to as Shelly (not her real name). Shelly was drawn to Beth right away, and they formed a close friendship. She told us that she wasn't sure if she was going to stay or follow Dr. John to his new location. She said that she had heard good things about the doctor that was going to replace him, and she wanted to meet her before making her decision. We followed her lead and decided we would do the same thing.

The first time we met Dr. Gale (not her real name), she was running about an hour behind schedule. We learned later that it was because she was spending extra time getting to know each patient. She wanted to learn as much about them as she could in that first meeting. When it was finally our turn, we were very impressed with her. Neither of us had ever met such a loving, caring physician. It didn't take long for us to realize that God knew what He was doing. We had needed Dr. John for his surgical skills, but we needed Dr. Gale for her genuine concern, knowledge and care at this point. Like everyone else, she fell in love with Beth because of her sweet disposition, positive attitude, and concern for others. Dr. Gale had mentioned early on that her father was in poor health. Beth never forgot, and she never failed to ask her how he was doing, because she did genuinely care.

After reviewing Beth's history, Dr. Gale said she thought Beth needed a break (especially her kidneys) from the chemo suites, so she prescribed a chemo pill. This seemed more like a vacation than a break. Beth experienced very little in the way of side effects from this pill and started to feel normal again. She was able to enjoy her favorite things, like shopping and going to lunch with her daughters and grandkids. It was great to see her feeling better, and on top of that, we only had to drive to Philadelphia once every three weeks for check-ups.

We gained a lot of time back in our daily lives. For a while, life was good. However, after a few months, we learned that the chemo pills, like the chemo injection treatments, had failed to shrink Beth's tumors. Once again, we got the report just before our summer vacation.

The chemo probably slowed the cancer down, but her tumors continued to grow. Dr. Gale remained optimistic in spite of the results of Beth's scan. Her positive attitude was contagious. We met with her just before leaving for our summer vacation. She told us to enjoy our vacation and not worry about the new treatment until we returned. Beth started crying during that appointment and asked Dr. Gale if she was running out of options. "Absolutely not!" she said. "We still have plenty of weapons in our arsenal. We are going to do everything in our power to shrink these tumors!"

I decided from that day forward that I would stay positive no matter what the scans revealed. I kept reminding Beth, and myself, that God was the great Physician and He could heal her at any time. We both believed that with all of our hearts.

Beth and I had always said that when I retired from QVC, we would do more traveling. Her cancer helped us realize that we needed to travel whenever we could and not wait for retirement. We planned a March vacation to visit our dear friends: Brian and Deb Roland. They lived in a cute, little community just outside of Pasadena, California. Brian is one of my oldest and dearest friends. He always says that I am the brother he never had, and I feel the same way about him. Beth and I were excited to escape the cold Philly weather for a few days and leave her chemo treatments behind.

When you are with great friends, you don't have to do anything exciting to have a great time. We enjoyed going to lunch and dinner, and just being together. One night we had dinner at a cool jazz club. Great food. Great music. Great friends. It was just a great vacation!

Beth and I had never been to a horse race track, so one afternoon Brian and Deb took us to Santa Anita Park. It was beautiful. We felt like we were living back in the 1950's when Bing Crosby and other famous people used to hang out here. The track has all the style and atmosphere from that era. We had so much fun trying to pick the winners of each race as the horses paraded by us. We were proud of the fact that we walked away with forty bucks in winnings from just one and two dollar bets on each race.

On the final day of our visit, Brian and Deb took us to

a fabulous restaurant called Nelson's, on the grounds of the beautiful Terranea Resort in Rancho Palos Verdes, California. The restaurant is on a cliff high above the Pacific Ocean, at the very spot where much of the popular television series *Sea Hunt* was filmed in the late fifties and early sixties—the owners named the restaurant after the lead character, Mike Nelson, who was played by Lloyd Bridges. The views of the ocean were breathtaking, and the food was delicious.

After lunch, we decided to walk through the lobby of the resort. As we were walking by the restaurant/bar area, Beth yelled, "There's John Tesh!" and pushed me through the door. John and his wife, Connie Sellecca, were sitting at a table playing *Rummikub* with Connie's mom.

I worked with John on QVC many times over the years. Beth was always a big fan of his, so I had him call her from the green room before one of our shows together. They hit it off fabulously on the phone! After about ten minutes, I said, "John you've talked long enough. I know you have other things to do."

He said, "Listen I'm enjoying talking to my new friend, Beth. You go prep for the show, and Beth and I will keep talking!" They talked for at least another half hour.

One of my fondest memories of my time as a host on QVC was when John and I spent a week together in Gisborne, New Zealand, for the Dawning of the New Millennium. We hosted a two-hour show from a beach on the shores of the Indian Ocean. Gisborne is known as "the City of First Light" because the first sunrise on the planet each day happens there. So, we were the very first people on earth to welcome in the new millennium a full eighteen hours ahead of New York!

John played a grand piano on a stage built on the beach just for the show. An indigenous Maori Indian tribe performed dances and added local flair to the show.

We rehearsed the show on December 31st and witnessed a breathtaking sunrise. However, when we woke up early in the morning on January 1st, 2000, a torrential downpour was in progress. Tons of work and lots of money had gone into this event and it appeared it was going to be rained out! John and I huddled with a few crew- members and held a prayer meeting in a tent on the beach about an hour before we were scheduled to go "live." By the start of the show, the rain started tapering off, and soon we witnessed yet another magnificent sunrise over the Indian Ocean. God heard and answered our prayers! It was an awe inspiring way to usher in the new millennium.

When the show was over, and we were packing up to leave, I asked John if he would sign one of his CDs for me as a memory of the show. He said he would be glad to do that, but he told me he had a much better gift. He picked up his keyboard and handed it to me. He said, "I know you're musically inclined so this is for you." I still have the keyboard, and I enjoy playing it.

It was a pleasure to run into John and Connie that day at the Terranea Resort. They were extraordinarily welcoming, and they seemed genuinely happy to see us. We talked for about twenty minutes when I finally said, "John, we need to leave you guys alone and let you get back to your family time."

He responded, "Do we look busy? We're just playing *Rummikub* and hanging out. It's fun catching up with you! Stick around a while!" He is an amiable, down- to- earth guy. His wife, Connie, is very kind and is even more beautiful in person than she is on television.

As we walked to our car, Deb said, "It's just not fair! Connie is so beautiful that it's not fair to the rest of us women on the planet!"

When we returned home from our California trip, we began looking forward to Kelsey's return home from Thailand. This trip was so good for her in so many ways. She shared many exciting experiences and showed us hundreds of pictures. She told us that the Lord helped her through many difficult times that strengthened her faith and deepened her walk with Him. We saw a new level of maturity in her when she returned home.

We were able to Skype with Kelsey on our computer several times while she was in Thailand. What a blessing it was to be able to see her and talk to her even though she was on the other side of the world! We met her Thai family, and she gave us a glimpse into her daily routine. We got a visual tour of the home she was living in and even saw a little bit of the city of Chang Mai.

Kelsey developed a love for the Thai people and their way of life. Her first week home she was missing Thai food, so she introduced us to her favorite dish, Mango and Sticky Rice. It is delicious!

Kelsey's stories gave our faith a boost. We could tell that she had matured not only emotionally but also spiritually while she was gone. In fact, she inspired our faith as we faced Beth's battle with cancer. At the same time, Beth and I were pleased and relieved to have our baby girl back home safely under our roof.

We had a wonderful time on our trip to California, and I still had some vacation time left, so we decided to go to Nashville for a four-day weekend in May. Kelsey was done with her semester and hadn't started her summer job yet, so she decided to come with us. I booked a suite at the Hilton Hotel in downtown Nashville right next door to the Country Music Hall of Fame.

Beth absolutely loved country music. We always tried to watch the *Country Music Awards* and the *Academy of Country Music Awards* on television. While she enjoyed all of the artists, her favorite, by far, was Keith Urban. She always got the biggest grin on her face whenever she saw him on television. I think she was secretly hoping we would run into him on the streets of Nashville. While that didn't happen, we still had a memorable time.

I had been to Nashville several times over the years for my work with QVC. I hosted two shows from a Nashville recording studio with country super group *Alabama*. I also hosted a show from the Music City celebrating the forty- year anniversary of the Corvette. I had promised Beth that I would take her to Nashville one day, and I finally got the chance.

One of my favorite Nashville hangouts is the World Famous Tootsie's Orchid Lounge located on Broadway in the heart of the city. It's a stone's throw away from the historic Ryman Auditorium where the Grand Ole Opry radio show began. Many country superstars sing at Tootsie's on their rise to stardom. You hear the very best country singers and musicians that you've never heard of, but probably will one day. And the music is free! They just pass a tip jar around through the crowd from time to time.

The music begins when they open their doors at 11 a.m. each day and goes nonstop until closing time at 2:30 a.m. The bands change out every few hours on three different stages. I'm always amazed at the high level of talent there. They perform for just those tips and the chance to be "discovered."

Tootsie's was our first stop once we arrived in town. Beth fell in love with it as soon as we walked in. We found a table on the second floor right beneath an imposing photo of Willie Nelson. I worked with Willie a couple of times on QVC; Beth and Kelsey both met him after one of the shows. He is one of the nicest, most mild mannered guys you could ever meet. He told me that Tootsie's was where he played a song he wrote called "Crazy" for Patsy Cline's husband because he wanted Patsy to record it. Her husband loved it, so they went and woke up Patsy and played it for her. The rest is history! Eventually, we were able to join some people at a table on the lower level with a much better view of the stage. We enjoyed appetizers and listened to music all afternoon. Beth was as happy as I've ever seen her. She leaned over and kissed me and told me she would be content to stay there and listen to the music all night long.

We toured the Country Music Hall of Fame the next morning.

It was truly a memorable experience. We walked through the entire history of country music! We especially enjoyed seeing video clips from the early country music television and radio shows like *HEE HAW*, the *Grand Ole Opry*, the *Glen Campbell Goodtime Hour* and others. Many of the displays featured the outfits worn by some of the most significant country music stars for their biggest performances. Being a musician, I loved seeing all of the guitars, banjos, fiddles and other instruments from famous recordings. One of Elvis' Cadillac sedans was on display, and it is huge! It appeared to be almost twice as long as many of today's compact cars. Huge plaques hang on the walls honoring every inductee of the Country Music Hall of Fame. We spent several hours there and still didn't see it all!

Beth wanted to go back to Tootsie's after we finished at the Hall of Fame. We listened to a couple of bands there and then walked a few blocks to another honky-tonk where people were singing and dancing. The strong sense of camaraderie in Nashville impressed us. It seemed like everyone knew every word to every song playing everywhere we went. The music definitely brings everyone together.

Another not-to-be-missed Nashville attraction if you get the chance: the Grand Ole Opry Theatre. We went on Saturday, May 17, 2014. We took the backstage tour before the show and enjoyed it immensely. They brought us into the green rooms and dressing rooms, and we got a feel for what the artists experience when they perform there. The best part was at the end of our tour when they took us onstage to have our picture taken by a professional photographer. Beth's face exudes a childlike joy in our photo, and I'll treasure it for the rest of my life.

The Grand Ole Opry Radio show broadcast was so much fun to watch. The show is produced "live" every Saturday from the Grand Ole Opry Theatre. It's the longest-running radio broadcast in US history. It features a mix of famous singers and contemporary artists who perform country, bluegrass, Americana, folk, and gospel. There are also comedic performances throughout. So one minute you're singing, and the next minute you're laughing.

The night we attended, Lauren Alaina was the headliner. She was the runner-up on season 10 of *American Idol*. Country music legends: Connie Smith, Little Jimmy Dickens and renowned mandolin player Sam Bush, performed, along with several other artists and entertainers. We had the time of our lives! It was indeed the perfect way to end our exciting time in Music City.

This was one of my all-time favorite vacations, mainly because Beth had a smile on her face from the moment we landed until the moment we left. As our plane took off, I wondered if we would ever come back.

Chemo treatments began again—every other week. Her creatinine level began running high—creatinine is a reflection of how well a person's kidneys are functioning. Because chemotherapy is hard on the kidneys, creatinine level is a number that chemo patients have to watch carefully. When Beth's creatinine was too high, she wasn't able to receive the treatment. I prayed before every treatment that her level would be low enough. There were several times, however, when it was indeed too high, so we had driven the seventy-four miles round trip for nothing. Those were just difficult days in the midst of an already difficult time … but Beth never let it get her down. She was still committed to enjoying every moment—and continuing to travel as long as she could.

11

$\mathcal{T}$he Outer Banks

We had heard that the Outer Banks of North Carolina were a beautiful vacation spot, but we had never been there. In June of 2014, we rented a large home for a week in Corolla, North Carolina. Once again, we went with our immediate family and Kirstyn's extended family. The house we rented had three levels. The top floor featured large windows facing in every direction, giving us a panoramic view of the entire area. To the east, we were greeted by the sunrise over the ocean every morning, and to the west, we watched the sunset over the bay every evening. It was the perfect vacation retreat.

The chemo treatments were beginning to take their toll on Beth. She was sleeping longer as her body tried to recuperate. Most days she didn't wake up until after eleven in the morning, so she was getting almost twelve hours of sleep each night. Since we wanted her to get plenty of rest, we didn't plan any family activities in the mornings. We usually just camped out on the beach under a tent in the afternoon. While we all wanted to stay out of the direct rays of the sun, Beth's doctor told her it was essential for *her* to do so. We enjoyed our family time together whether we were talking, reading or just watching the waves roll in. Cancer teaches you that the simple pleasures of life are indeed the best!

We brought plenty of groceries for breakfast and lunch. We took turns cooking dinner at night. Everybody had an evening to work on a team of two to three people who were responsible for dinner. They planned the meal, shopped for the groceries, prepared, served, and cleaned up the kitchen afterward. There were never any repeats, and everybody wanted theirs to be memorable. We had a little family competition going on, so everyone worked hard on the meals. After dinner we played lots of family games like *Charades*, *Win, Lose or Draw* or, our all-time favorite, *Trivial Pursuit*.

Vacations and family time became way more important to us after Beth's diagnosis. I enjoyed my time away from work much more because I realized that my time with Beth might be short. Before she got cancer, I was always in a hurry. I used to think if I wasn't always doing something "productive," I was wasting time. My attitude completely reversed after her diagnosis. Time became the most precious commodity I had. Beth, on the other hand, always knew how to enjoy each moment. She always told me that I should slow down and take more time to enjoy life. I finally took her advice.

We have a sitting room in our house located just to the right of our entryway. It is a cozy room with French doors leading into it. On one wall there is a breakfront that holds some unique dishes Beth collected and some family heirlooms. Other than that there are only a couch, a coffee table and a La-Z Boy chair in the room. Since there is no television, it's the perfect place for a good conversation. It was always Beth's favorite room. She loved to sit on the couch and drink her morning coffee. When I walked through she would often say to me, "Come sit by me for a while," as she patted the couch next to her. Many times through the years, I responded that I had too much to do, and I didn't have time to sit. After her cancer diagnosis, I ALWAYS stopped and sat with her. I made the time because I knew that time could be running out. Morning coffee with Beth became priority number one. I would certainly give anything now just to have a cup of coffee with her again.

Don't miss the simple moments with your loved ones, for there will come a time when you realize those simple moments were the most important moments of your life.

12

$\mathcal{I}$ Think I'll Dance

Beth and I loved to dance. It didn't matter where we were. If a great song was playing, we were usually dancing—fast and slow songs alike. We just had to dance!

After Kirstyn and Jeff's wedding on September 5, 2010, we threw a big party, with plenty of dancing. It had been a picture-perfect day for an outdoor wedding at the Downingtown Country Club in Downingtown, Pennsylvania. The reception followed afterward in a large banquet hall inside.

In the days leading up to the wedding, Beth and I had talked about the fact that this day would only happen once. We had put a lot of time and expense into it, so we decided we were going to enjoy every minute of it. This was two years before we found out she had cancer.

When they introduced the wedding party and the parents of the bride and groom, everybody came out dancing to their favorite song. The choice for Beth and me was a "no-brainer." Since we had met on September 21st, our favorite song was always "September" by Earth, Wind and Fire. When they introduced us, we came out dancing to that song, and we brought our best moves.

After dinner, it seemed like everybody hit the dance floor,

including my mom who had never danced in her entire life. She was eighty-eight years old at the time! I remember when she was dancing with Kelsey that she kept saying, "Oh my...this is fun!" Kirstyn wanted me to hire a deejay that she had heard at another wedding. He did a phenomenal job. Kirstyn picked the more current songs, and she let me pick the oldies. Since she grew up listening to the music that I picked, she was happy with my choices. Everybody kept dancing to the old and the new. The dance floor was packed, and Beth and I were right in the middle of it. We danced the night away!

L to R: Kelsey, Me, Cole, Kirstyn, Jeff, Beth
at Kirstyn's Wedding-Sept. 5, 2010.

The week after we returned from Nashville in May of 2014, the daughter of Deb Cortese, one of Beth's closest friends, got married. Her name is Cassie, and she had her wedding reception in a really cool looking barn in the Lancaster, Pennsylvania area. She had a deejay that played a lot of the music Beth and I loved, and once again we spent a lot of time on the dance floor.

Unfortunately, that was the last time Beth felt well enough to dance. Fortunately, the wedding photographer captured a lot of video of Beth and me dancing together (we were able to include that in the video presentation that we played at her Celebration of Life service).

From our earliest days together, Beth and I loved to dance. We were both big fans of Motown music and the mellow R&B music from the sixties and seventies. When she started to weaken from the chemo, we began dancing in my office at home. I have a vintage style radio/record player that I got from QVC. It is one of my all-time favorite products because it allowed me to play the albums that Beth and I grew up with. When she was too sick to go out we put on our favorite albums from our early years together and we slow danced. Just her and me, in my office, dancing to the music we grew up to and fell in love to. Those dances were the most meaningful to me.

In 1999, Lee Ann Womack recorded a song entitled, "I Hope You Dance." It was a smash hit and is considered to be her signature song. There is a line in that song that says, "And when you get the choice to sit it out or dance, I hope you dance." Beth and I always chose to dance. At her Celebration of Life service, one of the videos that my good friend Oscar Dovale put together honoring Beth's life featured a song called, "Dancing with the Angels" by Monk & Neagle. Kelsey suggested we use that song, and it was perfect. Along with lots of great pictures from Beth's life, Oscar was able to use the video of us dancing at Cassie's wedding. I'm sure that My Cakies is dancing in heaven right now.

Beth would want me to tell you to always remember that life is too short to sit it out. So, we hope you'll dance!!!

13

The Battle Rages

As we moved into the second half of 2014, it felt like we were moving into a much more difficult phase of Beth's fight. Her doctor decided to put her on a different chemo drug because the second combination of drugs wasn't containing the tumors. We were still hopeful at this point, but our concern was growing. Although most people handled this new drug very well, Beth turned out to be an exception. She experienced more nausea and achiness than ever. I was beginning to worry that if this drug didn't work, it might be over. Deep in my heart, I knew God was still in control. But I also knew we needed a miracle soon!

My younger sister, Dawn, came to visit in late July along with her husband, Glenn, and their daughter, Abbey. I think they realized that they had better come and see Beth while she still felt good enough to have company. They are fun-loving people. Glenn is one of those guys who can find humor in everything. The Bible says that **"a merry heart doeth good like a medicine."-Proverbs 17:22, King James Version of the Bible.** Beth and I got a good strong dose of that medicine during their visit. They kept things light and lifted our spirits. It was one of the highlights of the summer.

Another friend of ours, named Buck, was fighting cancer

at this time. Buck worked at QVC as a videographer. He was a happy, upbeat guy; working with him was always a pleasure. We worked on several projects together during my QVC career. He and his family lived in the first neighborhood we lived in when we moved to Pennsylvania in 1991. They had a daughter who was Kelsey's age, so we often ran into Buck and his family at school-related events.

Buck was well liked and well respected by everyone. It was extremely difficult for those of us who knew him and worked with him to watch his illness wear him down physically. Early in the summer of 2014, I noticed that he was losing weight rather quickly. He appeared to be very tired, but he kept working hard. I'll never forget running into him in the atrium at QVC one day when he showed off his new chemo pack that he was wearing on his belt. He said, "Wheels, this is the coolest thing ever. It's chemo to go!" He always looked at the positive side of every situation.

One day in early August, I ran into one of Buck's fellow videographers on my way into the studio. When I asked about Buck, he told me the sad news that he had passed away that morning. It hit me hard.

I attended the viewing and funeral service on August 15th. It was hard to say goodbye to Buck and in the back of my mind, I wondered if I would be attending a similar service for Beth in the near future.

A few months later, in November, Kelsey put on a fundraising event for her college senior project. Blue Sky Band (the charity band I have played in for over 14 years) performed, and I was able to help her with a silent auction. It was a big success! Her goal was to raise $1,000 for the Bridge Academy Community Center (BACC) in Coatesville, Pennsylvania. This event raised more than twice that amount! Kelsey has volunteered there since she was in the eighth grade. She has worked faithfully with children from difficult family backgrounds for more than twelve years. I am so proud of her faithfulness and dedication.

This fundraiser was important to Kelsey, and she wanted her mom to be there. Beth knew it was a big deal to her, so she rested up and came out. Many of our friends were there, and they were all thrilled to see her. As the event concluded and I was packing up my band gear, Beth asked me if we could stay and have dinner with a few of the friends who were there. Of course, I said, "Yes!" I learned early on in this journey that when Beth felt well enough to go, we needed to go with it and have fun! It was one of those nights where we enjoyed a great meal and then stayed at the table until the restaurant kicked us out!

About a week before Christmas, we flew Beth's mom, Elaine, out from Chicago to stay with us for the holidays. She always loved coming out and spending time with our family, especially Beth. Beth was extremely close with her mom. She was feeling pretty good because her doctor, once again, gave her a break from the chemo so she could enjoy the holidays. We did indeed. It was one of the best Christmas seasons ever!

Beth and her mom, Elaine Johnson-December 2012.

As 2014 came to a close, I felt in my spirit that 2015 was going to be a challenging year. It seemed like Beth's battle was intensifying. The tumors in her abdomen kept growing, and the chemo was wearing her body down.

In the early days of January, I met with my scheduler at QVC (a wonderful woman named Mary Harlyvetch) to ask if I could get taken off some of the weekend night shifts. Since Beth's health was deteriorating more rapidly, I didn't know how many weekend evenings we had left at this point. Mary very graciously said that she would work with me so that I could have some of those evenings with Beth. Thank you, Mary!

QVC was very good to me throughout Beth's entire three-year fight with cancer. I was extremely fortunate to work for such a wonderful company. I felt wholly supported by everyone who worked there.

At this time, Beth was receiving her chemo treatments every other week, so she didn't have much time to recover between sessions. While she always did her absolute best to keep her spirits up, it was apparent that the chemo was taking a heavy toll. One night as we were getting ready for bed, she told me that it was getting harder and harder to go through the treatments. I began to wonder how much longer she would make it. Honestly, I don't know how she did it as long as she did. Her undying love for her family and friends and her strong will to live kept her going.

14

Sadie, Lacie and Zoey

Beth loved animals almost as much as people. We had a cute, little white Bichon dog named Sadie and a beautiful, Siamese cat named Lacie. Beth had been a major cat lover since childhood, so we always had one or two cats around. Sadie, however, was our first dog.

Kelsey's "dogged" persistence was the main reason we had Sadie. When Kelsey was twelve years old, she suddenly developed an incredibly strong desire to have a puppy. Strong is probably not a "strong" enough word. She began asking me for a dog every day and didn't give up after a week or two as most kids would. She kept asking every day for an entire year! One day she wrote me a very long letter begging and pleading with me to let her get a puppy. She promised that she would take care of it and that I wouldn't have to worry about a thing.

Beth may have been in on this, because she began researching what type of dog we should get. The Bichon breed rose to the top of the list because they don't shed. As Beth had asthma, this was very important.

I finally gave in and agreed to get a puppy. Beth and the girls wasted no time finding an adorable female Bichon. Kelsey named her Sadie, and we all fell in love with her. She was a well- behaved puppy with the sweetest disposition ever. We loved her, and she loved us back unconditionally for ten years. Every time we entered the house this little, fluffy white dog would greet us with barks of sheer delight. She wagged her tail so hard that her whole body moved from side to side. Don't you wish people got that excited to see you?

One day in early January of 2015, we noticed Sadie was having trouble walking. We took her to the veterinarian's office, and after conducting several x-rays and scans, the vet found our precious pup had a tumor wrapped around her spinal cord. It was too dangerous to operate. Beth and I had to make the gut-wrenching decision to have her put to sleep. I will never forget that day. We held her little face in our hands during the injection and wept as we said our goodbyes. It was one of the saddest days of our lives. Fortunately, Kelsey was away at college.

Sadie had been Beth's lap dog. She kept her company throughout her illness and always cuddled with her on the bed or couch. After we put her down, the house seemed too quiet. We missed the sound of her paws on our wood floors. We missed being greeted at the door by her wagging tail and welcoming kisses. I knew I had to find another white Bichon and I had to find one soon.

One day I took Beth to Mannheim, Pennsylvania, where I had found another female bichon online; she looked a lot like Sadie in her photographs. When we saw her in person, we knew she was our dog. We named her Zoey. She is more rambunctious than Sadie but just as sweet! We fell in love all over again.

15

More Cancer in Our Family

My daughter Kirstyn's husband Jeff is a terrific young man, who comes from a happy, loving family. We were all devastated to learn that Jeff's father Ed had throat cancer. Most people assume throat cancer comes from smoking but Ed was not a smoker! It was early spring; Beth's battle with cancer was already intense … and now this. Our family was reeling.

Ed had to have surgery, followed by numerous radiation treatments. At this point, both Jeff and Kirstyn each had a parent who was fighting cancer. Ed went through a lot, as they hit the cancer often and hard with the radiation. Fortunately, the treatments were effective, and later that year Ed was declared to be cancer- free.

Beth's tumors, however, continued to grow regardless of the amount or type of chemo drugs her doctor prescribed. By mid-March she was experiencing a lot of pain and pressure in her pelvic region. A scan revealed that one of her tumors had grown so much that it was pressing on her ureter. The ureter is the duct by which urine passes from the kidney to the bladder. Beth's urologist explained he could put in a stint to help relieve the pressure. We agreed to have the procedure done at an outpatient facility near our house. The surgery went well, and Beth began experiencing relief immediately.

That evening we were relaxing at home when she suddenly had a craving for orange sherbet. I immediately left the house to go on a search. I visited three different grocery stores before I found it, but I'm so glad I did! It tasted great, and made Beth so very happy. It never took much. She truly loved the simplest things in life! The Joy of the Lord was her strength. She loved her life and everyone in it.

When I triumphantly returned home with the orange sherbet, Beth was on the phone with her cousin, Mark Johnson. She hadn't talked to Mark in many years, so she enjoyed catching up with him. Mark heard about Beth's illness and apologized to her for not staying in touch as well as he would have wanted. They talked for well over an hour. That was the last time they spoke.

Who do you need to call? You may not get another chance to speak to that person, so if somebody comes to mind, call them today!

16

Making Memories through the Pain

A week later, Kirstyn and Kelsey took their mom to see Miranda Lambert in concert in Atlantic City, New Jersey. They made it a girls' weekend, and stayed overnight at a beautiful hotel. When they came home, Beth told me she enjoyed the concert and loved her time with our girls. Recently, I looked at a picture of the three of them at that concert, and even though Beth was smiling, I could see in her face that she wasn't feeling well. She didn't want to miss a chance to make a memory with her girls, regardless of the pain. Kirstyn and Kelsey will always treasure the memory of being with their mom at that concert.

As May approached, we began looking forward to Kelsey's graduation from Messiah College. Mother's Day fell on the Sunday before, and I made plans to take our family out to brunch after church to celebrate. Unfortunately, Beth felt so ill she couldn't get out of bed. I canceled our reservation for brunch, and worked out in the yard most of the day. I made sure to check on her every hour. Around 6 p.m., she got up and came outside to ask if I wanted to go down to our favorite little diner for dinner. I told her I would go only if she promised me that she felt well enough. She said she did. Looking back I know she went just for me. She was the most unselfish person I have ever known. Even in her worst pain, she was thinking of me. She knew I wanted to celebrate Mother's Day with her, so she was determined at least to go to our favorite diner.

With the same determination, Beth would let absolutely nothing keep her from attending Kelsey's college graduation the following Saturday. It was a hot, humid, summer-like day on May 16th and, of course, the ceremony was outside. Since Beth had lost all of her hair, she had to wear a scarf on her head to help keep her cool and prevent sunburn. Her medications made her feel warm even when it was cool outside, so I knew she would be uncomfortable sitting in the sun for the entire ceremony.

Kirstyn had graduated seven years earlier from Messiah, and, of course, she came to celebrate Kelsey's accomplishment. She brought her oldest son, Cole, who was five years old at the time.

There weren't any seats in the shade, so we got as close to the stage as possible. As soon as we sat down, we started looking at the program for Kelsey's name. When we found it, we noticed there was an asterisk by her name that denoted she was graduating with honors. That was one the hardest earned asterisks ever! If you knew how hard Kelsey worked to achieve this, you would understand why Beth was so determined to be there. On this day she received her undergraduate degree in Social Work. Kelsey has always had a strong desire to help people less fortunate than her.

Kelsey had a tough time in grade school due to a learning disability that involved short-term memory loss. We had her tested at a prestigious college when she was in the third grade. When we got the results, Beth insisted that we get her extra help right away. I had tried to help her with her homework up to this point, but ultimately it was a much more significant challenge than I could handle.

Kelsey loved her third-grade teacher, and so did we. Her name was Michelle. She was precisely the person that Kelsey needed. Michelle was extremely patient and kind. She agreed to come to our home and work with Kelsey for several hours after school once a week. She did this faithfully from the third through the sixth grade—and turned around Kelsey's academic career and her future. It was the best investment we ever made. Kelsey learned how to work hard and study effectively.

Her persistence and determination, along with her tutor's patience, brought her to this day, when she graduated with honors from a highly rated and well-respected college. As we sat waiting for the graduation ceremonies to begin, Beth and I reminisced about those difficult times when she was in elementary school. We never imagined this day back then. We were, obviously, as proud of her as we could be, just as we were when Kirstyn graduated seven years earlier. Beth told me later how grateful she was to be able to attend both of our girls' college graduations.

School had been a challenge for Beth, too. She struggled with reading in grade school, but never got the help she needed. As a result, she never liked school and didn't go to college. She wanted to make sure that didn't happen to Kelsey. She wanted her to have all the opportunities that her mother didn't have. There were many times when we wondered if Kelsey would make it through high school, let alone college. But she did it! Beth's love for Kelsey propelled her to find the answer to her learning challenges. **If you have a child who needs extra help with their schoolwork, please get them the help they need. It will make a huge difference in their life. You will never regret it!**

We took a couple of group pictures at Commencement, but then we moved to individual photos of each of us with Kelsey in her cap and gown. The picture of Beth and Kelsey was especially meaningful. The following Christmas, Kirstyn had that picture framed, and the caption reads, "If ever there comes a day when we can't be together, keep me in your heart, I'll stay there forever." That quote is from *Winnie the Pooh*, written by A. A. Milne. Kelsey loved the photo and caption. A year later when she received her master's degree in Social Work from West Chester University, Beth wasn't physically in the graduation photo, but that picture was. Kelsey was holding it.

Kelsey and Beth at Kelsey's college graduation-May, 2015.

Just eight days after Kelsey's graduation from Messiah, we had to rush Beth to the hospital once again. She had severe abdominal pain, and her pain medication failed to give her any relief. At two o'clock in the morning, they transferred her from our suburban hospital to the one in downtown Philadelphia where she'd had her first surgery.

After a couple of days of x-rays and scans, Dr. Gale and her associates determined that the tumor that was causing Beth so much pain was composed mainly of fluid. She walked into Beth's hospital room and told us she was pretty confident they would be able to drain the tumor and give Beth a lot of relief. Dr. Gale looked at me and said that I could take her home that evening.

Pain never stopped Beth's hurricane of love. She spread it around to all the nurses, nursing assistants, technicians, physician's assistants and doctors in every hospital and medical facility. True to her form, she always worried about everybody else more than herself. Here's another example of her unselfish love. I was scheduled to fly to Milwaukee on Thursday of this week to visit my then ninety-three year old mother. When Beth was admitted to the hospital on that Sunday, however, I told her I was going to cancel my trip. She asked me to wait and see how she was doing on Wednesday before I canceled. After Doctor Gale told us I could take her home on Wednesday evening, Beth looked at her and said, "Will you tell my husband to go visit his ninety-three year old mom in Milwaukee tomorrow?" Dr. Gale complied and assured me that Beth would be okay and that I should go. Beth remained unselfish throughout her battle with cancer. She knew how disappointed my mom would have been if I couldn't go, and she wouldn't let me miss the chance to see my elderly mother.

Beth's niece, Lisa, was scheduled to bring her family for a weeklong visit on June 15th. She and her husband, Jim, were flying in from San Francisco along with their two boys, Jake and Ryan. Beth had been looking forward to this for months, so I wanted everything to go smoothly. I worked extra hard to make sure that the yard and the pool area were in tip-top shape by the time they arrived. My biggest fear was that Beth wouldn't feel good enough to enjoy their visit. As it turned out, we had a phenomenal time. Our grandsons, Cole and Gavin, absolutely loved hanging out with their older cousins. We made up several mattresses and put them on the basement floor so all the boys could sleep together. We joked that they had their own little dormitory down there. Cole wanted to stay at our house the entire week. After a few nights, Kirstyn begged him to come home and sleep in his bed for one night because she missed him. He agreed but made her promise that it would only be for one night.

June was unusually warm that year, so we were able to swim in the pool every day and unwind in the hot tub every night. We made s'mores in the fire pit and sang songs by the fire. But I think Jake and Ryan's favorite memory was catching fireflies in a glass jar. This was a regular summer activity for me while I was growing up in Michigan, but Jake and Ryan had never seen fireflies in Northern California where they lived. They were utterly mesmerized watching them light up our backyard on those warm summer evenings. I showed them how to poke holes in the jar lid so the fireflies could get air while they were confined. Of course, we let them all fly away after a short time. This brought back many great childhood memories for the adults.

Whenever family and friends visited us, they wanted to see QVC. So one night, I took them all on a tour of the studios. Giving QVC tours always reminded me what a fantastic place it is and how fortunate I was to work there as a Program Host for twenty-nine years. The studios are absolutely beautiful, and it is exciting to watch the broadcast team in action as they execute such a complicated show. They do it twenty-four hours a day, and they do it better than anybody else. It is impressive! **If you are ever in the West Chester area, you should seriously consider taking the QVC Studio Tour.**

We took a lot of family pictures during that week. When I look at them now, I can tell that Beth wasn't feeling well at all. She did her best to disguise it and somehow still managed to be the ultimate host. By this point, however, her tumors were continually causing her pain and discomfort. After Lisa, Jim and the boys left, Beth's other niece from California, Kim Bellone and her husband, Chris, came by and spent the day with us. We hung out, watched soccer and made a delicious dinner. Beth was very surprised and very happy!

July started out with Beth needing two more stints in her ureter to control the pressure from other tumors. As she was being prepped for the procedure, I was sitting in a chair next to her bed. The nurse accidentally lowered the bed very suddenly, and it came down full force on both of my knees! It hurt like crazy, and I let out a yell. Beth thought it was hilarious. Fortunately, the pain left quickly, and I had no lasting damage, but I played it up to make her laugh even more. As caring and empathetic as she was it always struck her funny bone whenever I got hurt. She tried to tell me that it was a nervous reaction that expressed itself in the form of laughter. I'm not sure that I believe that. But I was happy that I could still make her laugh (even if it meant a little pain).

Our family had another beach getaway on the calendar for the following week, but Beth and I hadn't planned to go because of Beth's health. The rental house had an extra room for us, and it was only a two-hour drive, so we decided to go down for just a few days in the middle of the week. At this point, Beth had trouble sitting in the heat, even under a canopy. She and I usually came back to the house early in the afternoon to rest up before dinner. She enjoyed sitting on the deck in the evening because there was always a warm ocean breeze. We had missed out on the early part of the week, so we stayed later than anyone else—and we were the ones who dropped the keys off to the realtor on the last morning. On the drive home, I wondered if that would be the last beach vacation for Beth and me together.

17

The Little Things are the BIG Things

The rest of July was filled with doctor's appointments and even more procedures. On July 30th I took Beth into downtown Philly to have her tumor drained. We didn't know how much fluid was in the tumor, but her doctor was hopeful they would drain a significant amount. Kirstyn drove down to be with us. We stayed with Beth while they prepped her, and then made our way to the waiting area. Kirstyn and I prayed together, and then she had to leave to pick up Cole from school.

I remember how utterly alone I felt in that waiting room after she left. Since I was the only person there, I knelt by a chair and prayed during the entire procedure. When they called me in afterward, the doctor informed me that they had drained two liters of fluid from the tumor. That is the size of a large bottle of soda pop! I was so thankful because I knew this would give Beth quite a bit of relief. I didn't know how long her relief would last, but I believe God answered my prayers that day.

By August, it was evident that the many procedures and treatments were weakening Beth's body. Somehow she still kept her spirits high every day.

One day in early August, I was scheduled to rehearse with a major celebrity, who is well known around the world, to help her get ready for her QVC appearance that evening. I'll call her Lynn (not her real name). After years of working with celebrities, I felt confident that I could help prepare her for a great airing. When I walked into the studio that afternoon, about twenty people were standing around talking to each other. Lynn was standing alone in a corner. When I asked one of the producers what was going on, she told me that Lynn was having reservations about the rehearsal. It appeared to me that there were way too many people in the studio, so I asked everyone to leave except for her.

As soon as the crowd was gone, I looked at her and said, "It is an honor to meet you. We're delighted that you are here, and if you don't want to rehearse we don't have to." She was very polite, but she didn't understand why we needed a rehearsal. I explained to her that what we did at QVC was very different from other television shows and that the rehearsal would help to prepare her. I explained that we just wanted her to get used to the format. I added, "However, if you don't want to do it, you don't have to." For whatever reason, I then began to tell her about Beth. I remember saying something like, "This rehearsal isn't that important, but I'll tell you what is. My wife has stage 4 cancer and probably doesn't have long to live. She is way more important to me than this rehearsal, and I would much rather be home with her right now. However, since you and I are both here, it would be nice if we could just run through your presentation a couple of times since we have the crew here."

When I finished talking, Lynn said, "Dan, I am so sorry for what you are going through, and I would very much like to run through this presentation with you." I called everyone back into the studio, and we spent the next hour rehearsing. She did a tremendous job.

When we finished, she hugged me and asked if I would be around when she came back in later that evening. I told her that I would, since I would be on the air until 10 p.m. She asked me to stop by her green room after my shift because she had something that she wanted to give to Beth.

After my show, I stuck my head into her green room. She invited me in, and thanked me for helping her with the rehearsal. She then handed me a sealed packet, and asked me to give it to Beth. She told me she had written her a letter, and included a booklet that she might enjoy.

When I arrived home that night, I told Beth that I had a present for her from this major international celebrity. She opened the packet, and read a very compassionate and loving handwritten letter. She told Beth that she was so sorry for what she was going through, but that she knew she was very strong and well loved. She wanted Beth to know that she would be praying for her, and thinking about her in the days to come. Along with the note, was a beautiful pictorial filled with magnificent pictures of the place where this celebrity lived. The land is filled with flowering trees and magnificent gardens. She wrote by each photo why it was a special place to her, and that she hoped Beth would find comfort in looking at the pictures from time to time. We were both touched by her kindness. She obviously put a lot of time and thought into this, and it meant a lot to both of us. Celebrities are real people with real feelings like you and me. I have learned that they need to be spoken to like normal people.

Beth and I didn't talk about it much, but we both knew our time was growing short. We rarely left our house that summer, and spent many afternoons just sitting on lounge chairs by the pool holding hands. We talked about heaven, and tried to imagine what it would be like. Sometimes we reminisced about happier times. At times we didn't talk at all. We were together, and that was enough.

Many days we sat there all afternoon and watched the sun go down. We listened to the birds. We noticed they began to sing more as the evening approached. Many times we were still sitting and holding hands in the dark. Eventually, we got up and went into the house. I'll never forget those days for they were among the most precious days of my life. Cakies and I were together, just being, just holding hands and savoring every minute. Oh, what I would give to have even one of those afternoons back. I will always treasure the summer of 2015. Even though it was one of the most difficult and challenging times of my life, it was also the most meaningful. We honestly had our priorities in the right place.

I still go outside sometimes on summer afternoons, and sit on the lounger that I always sat in that summer. I pretend that Beth is sitting in the other one, and I watch the sun go down. I sit in the dark for a while before I go in the house for the evening, and I wonder what she's doing in heaven.

Take time to sit with your spouse, your child, your sibling, your parent or your friend. Don't miss life's precious moments. Don't miss the chance just to be together........... while you can.

18

A Party of Two

During one of our meetings with Dr. Gale that summer we were discussing Beth's pain and how it had increased. I asked if medical marijuana might help to lessen the intensity of her pain. Dr. Gale thought it might, so she wrote Beth a prescription for it.

One day, unbeknownst to me, Beth took one of the pills. I was sitting next to her underneath an umbrella by the pool when her mom called. I noticed Beth wasn't saying much. Beth and her mom are usually very talkative on the phone, so this seemed strange. As she hung up, I saw her eyes looked glassy. I said, "Cakies are you alright?"

She responded, "I think I'm high! I took a medical marijuana pill!" The next thing I know she starts playing music on her phone and gets up and starts dancing. She was singing and laughing hysterically. I pulled out my phone and began recording video. I wanted Kirstyn and Kelsey to see their mom having fun. At one point, Beth walked up to me and just fell into my arms and started dancing with me. We danced and laughed together for several minutes. She was having the time of her life! It was our own little party. The fun lasted for about fifteen minutes and then she flopped down onto a lounger and fell asleep. I covered her with a large beach towel and let her sleep it off.

Since my office looks out toward the pool area, I decided to make a few doctor's appointments for her and catch up on paying bills while keeping an eye on her. I went out to check on her about an hour and a half later. I quietly whispered her name a few times. She eventually opened her eyes and said, "I want a cheese pizza from Joey's now!" I told her I was on my way to get one. As I ordered the pizza from my car, I started laughing out loud because she had all the classic symptoms of being high. She danced, she laughed at everything, slept it off and woke up with the munchies! She wanted pizza from our favorite neighborhood cheesesteak and pizza place and I was going to get it for her.

When I returned with the pizza, she opened the box and quickly ate three pieces. That was the most she had eaten in weeks. As the effects of the drug wore off, she told me that for three hours she forgot she had cancer. I thought to myself, "Thank God for medical marijuana. It helped her to forget about the cancer, the pain, and the chemo. It helped her laugh and have fun for a few short hours."

My friends and co-workers rallied around me at this time. My boss, Jack Comstock, often called me at the beginning of the week to ask how things were going. I remember one time when he called I told him that she was still fighting hard, but that her body was wearing down. He then asked how I was doing, and I said I was hanging in there and that I would be able to do my on-air shifts that week. He responded, "No, I have taken you off the schedule this week. The other hosts can cover your timeslots. You need to be home with Beth." I hung up and thanked the Lord for giving me such an understanding and caring boss. I was also thankful for the great team of hosts I worked with at QVC who were willing to work extra shifts so that I could take care of my wife.

My sister, Margie Lou, my brother-in-law, George and my mom drove out to see us in the middle of August. I had told them that if they wanted to see Beth, they needed to come right away.

I'm glad they did. Beth tried to spend a lot of time with them in spite of the fact she had severe abdominal pain. She somehow was able to go out for lunch a couple of times during their visit. We even went out for Beth's favorite treat, ice cream.

Margie Lou always loved to visit the QVC Outlet store when they came out. She loves to shop! So all of us, including Beth, went shopping there one afternoon. Beth had frequented the store many times through the years but hadn't been there for a long time. Everybody who worked there loved her, and they were very excited to see her when she walked in.

The daughter of one of Beth's closest friends was getting married that Friday. We had looked forward to the wedding since spring. The bride's name was Cindy Dickey. Kirstyn and Cindy were lifelong friends. They started playing soccer together when they were just six years old. We had enjoyed going to their games and became good friends with many of the parents. Beth always put a big pink bow in Kirstyn's hair so we could easily spot her on the field. As the girls got older, they played on a travel team together. We spent many weekends watching them play soccer. The parents all became close on weekend trips to tournaments. Beth became best of friends with Cindy's mom, Sherry.

Since Beth had been feeling so poorly, I wasn't sure if we would be attending the wedding. Beth was determined to go so we got all dressed up. I'll never forget how beautiful Beth looked even without her hair. George took our picture together before we left. I'm glad he did. I treasure that picture because it was the last time we dressed up for a date.

The wedding ceremony was outdoors, and the weather cooperated: a picture-perfect summer evening. A reception and dinner followed inside the country club where the wedding took place. Beth made it through the ceremony fine, but just before dinner, she asked if I could run out to the car to get her a pain pill. She had fooled even me up to that point because she had been smiling, laughing and complimenting everyone in the wedding party. She acted like she felt on top of the world. After dinner, they opened up the dance floor. Beth tried to dance for a song or two but didn't feel well enough; I didn't mind, because I was just happy she was by my side. Jeff and Kirstyn were there, and we all wore colors that matched. We took a great photo of the four of us at the reception.

Throughout the next afternoon and evening, Beth had trouble controlling her pain. She felt better moving than sitting, so she kept walking around the pool. Margie, George, Kelsey, and I went on a very long walk with Beth that evening, so she felt a little relief. We had a long list of prescription pain medications, but nothing seemed to help that night.

We were in constant contact with Beth's doctor and her physician's assistant by phone at this time. They realized that her pain was getting harder to manage, so they suggested that we begin palliative care. This type of care grew out of the hospice movement. People suffering from serious and chronic illnesses such as cancer are eligible to receive it. We had a care team consisting of a social worker, chaplain, and a few specialized nurses. They came to our home several times a week to help us manage Beth's pain.

Our first in-home visit was on Wednesday, August 26th. The nurse was very friendly. She taught me how to give Beth pain injections at home. The first week went well. However, later in the week, we got a call from Shelly, our physician's assistant. She said that Dr. Gale wanted us to see a pain doctor. They said they wanted an objective opinion because they were both so close to Beth. When I heard that, a huge red flag went up in my mind. I wondered what the ultimate objective of this meeting was.

A pain doctor, naturally, specializes in managing pain. This doctor was very cordial. She asked Beth all about her pain and how she was managing it. Near the end of the meeting, she told us that we should think about stopping treatment and transitioning to hospice care. Hearing the word "hospice" sent chills down my spine. To me, hospice meant it was the end. It meant that we were waving the white flag of surrender.

As we left her office and started down the elevator, I asked Beth what she thought about the meeting. She said that she was angry that this doctor suggested hospice. She said she wasn't ready to give up and that she wanted to keep fighting and continue treatment. I said, "OK! We will call Dr. Gale and tell her to schedule our next chemo treatment." I was glad that she wanted to keep fighting!

Dr. Gale told us we should wait until later in the month to start the next drug. She felt like Beth's kidneys needed a break. In the meantime, the palliative care nurse suggested that Beth wear a pain pack so she could disperse the medicine as soon as she felt the pain coming on. It was a small pack about the size of a paperback novel that they could attach directly to her port. It had a strap that enabled her to wear it across her body like some women's handbags. Whenever the pain started, Beth could simply press a button and receive the medication instantly. It worked extremely well. Beth felt so good the first week she had it that she went shopping with Kirstyn and Kelsey and went out for lunch a couple of times. We were all excited that her pain was under control. She seemed happy and relieved.

It was now the second week in September so it was time to close the pool for the season. Every May we celebrated when the pool opened and every September we were sad when it closed. I was extra sad this year because I didn't know if Beth would be with us when it opened again in spring.

My son-in-law, Jeff, coached special teams for a local high school football team, so we always enjoyed going to the team's home games in the fall. On Friday, September 18th Beth and I went to the game and sat with Kirstyn, Cole, and Gavin. It was a beautiful Friday night, and we stayed until well into the second half. It felt great to be out of the house on a date with my Cakies.

I took a selfie of us sitting in the stands that night. I'm so glad I did because it was the last football game we attended together.

The next day, our friends, Bryan and Kim Law, called and asked if we could go down to the shore with them for the rest of the weekend. Beth was tired, but she thought it would be nice to go down early Sunday morning and come back Monday afternoon. Again, I'm so glad we did.

We drove down to Sea Isle City, New Jersey and met them for lunch at an outdoor café on the beach. It was a beautiful afternoon, and we enjoyed a great seafood lunch overlooking the ocean. When we got back to their beach house, Beth was tired and took a long nap in the bedroom. When she woke up, it was time for dinner. Bryan and Kim took us to a quaint little seafood restaurant that had a lobster special going on. Beth loved lobster, and I'll never forget how much she enjoyed that meal. She kept saying it was the best lobster she had ever tasted! The only thing that Beth loved more than lobster was ice cream! So, after dinner, we found a place that served homemade ice cream. We ate our cones outside and walked around the downtown area of Sea Isle. It was a perfect day and night, and it turned out to be Beth's last trip to the shore.

Enjoy life's simple pleasures. Life is short. Go to high school football games. Drive down to the shore. Eat lobster and, whatever you do, don't forget to eat the ice cream!

19

$\mathcal{T}$he Beginning of the End

Beth was scheduled to have her next chemo treatment on Tuesday, September 22nd. They started her on another new drug that we were told most people tolerated well. I don't know exactly how many different chemo drugs they tried, but I was always hopeful when we started a new one. We didn't realize it at the time, but this would be her last treatment and our last chemo suite date.

I went directly to the bakery when we arrived, and Beth went upstairs to sign in for her doctor's appointment. Her checkup went well, and her creatinine level was just low enough for her to get the green light for the chemo.

Each new drug had to be approved by our insurance company. As we settled into the chemo suite, our nurse told us that there was a hold up because the insurance company had denied coverage for the new drug. The insurance company questioned why this new drug was being used to treat Beth's type of cancer, as it was usually used for other types. This had happened before, and we knew that the hospital would resubmit the request with more information from Beth's doctor.

Our nurse told us she was going to go ahead and start Beth on the fluids with the hope that the insurance company would approve the drug. Beth began to panic, but for some reason, I stayed calm. I told her that if she was supposed to get this drug, it would get approved and if not we would get to go home early and come back another time. As soon as they finished with the fluids, the nurse came in with the new drug and said, "It's been approved."

Because of all the delays, it was a very long day. We didn't return home until after seven that night. We were both exhausted and went to bed early.

The next day Beth woke up feeling good. I brought her coffee and muffins while she was still in bed. It was a beautiful day, so we lingered a while drinking our coffee and enjoying the view out our bedroom window. Kirstyn called to see how her mom was feeling, and when Beth told her she felt good, Kirstyn suggested they do something fun with the grandsons. I had to work that afternoon and evening, so I was glad they were going to spend the afternoon together.

Beth and Kirstyn decided to take Cole and Gavin to a place by our home called Highland Orchards. It has always been a favorite spot for our family. Our girls loved going there as they were growing up, and Kirstyn has continued that tradition with her kids. The orchard sells farm fresh fruits and vegetables, along with delicious homemade pies and donuts. We always went there in the fall to pick out our pumpkins.

We learned early on in Beth's fight with cancer that when she felt well, we needed to take advantage of it and enjoy the day to the fullest. That is what Kirstyn and Beth decided to do on this day. They spent the entire afternoon at Highland Orchards. They got pumpkins, ate lunch outside, and fed the goats. Beth was feeling so good that she played with her grandsons on the playground. Kirstyn later wrote on her Facebook page that she loved watching her mom catch Gavin at the bottom of the slide and push Cole on the swings. Kirstyn wanted to capture a picture to remember the beautiful fun day they had so she talked

Beth into taking a selfie. That picture became one of Kirstyn's favorites.

Beth had a super relationship with our girls. Kirstyn and Kelsey both considered her to be their best friend. She had a special and unique bond with both of them. When Kirstyn became a mom, she learned from the best. Beth was able to teach her so much about taking care of babies. Being a mom came naturally to Beth because she had so much love to give. She was able to keep her authority as a mom even though she also became "best friends" with her daughters. Somehow she always maintained that perfect balance. Being a grandma to our grandsons came as naturally for her. She was the rock of our family. She was the glue that held us together. Our son-in-law, Jeff, affectionately called her "The Matriarch of Our Family."

L to R: Kelsey, Kirstyn and Beth at Kirstyn's wedding- September 5, 2010.

On Friday, September 25th, I played with Blue Sky Band at a hotel ballroom in Malvern, Pennsylvania. It was a fundraiser for Cystic Fibrosis. I worked all day starting at 10 a.m. and ending with a two-hour food show from 4 p.m. to 6 p.m. When I finished, I drove directly to the fundraiser because we were supposed to start playing at 7:15 p.m., and the hotel was about twenty minutes away from work. As usual, I called Beth on my way to the gig. She sounded good. In fact, she said that she seemed to be handling the new chemo drug pretty well and hadn't felt any adverse side effects yet. This was good news!

The fundraiser was a big success, and Blue Sky band had played one of our best gigs ever. By the time we packed up all of our equipment it was after 11 p.m. I was exhausted after a long day and was looking forward to crawling into bed.

When I called home to tell Beth I was on my way home I immediately knew something was wrong. When she answered the phone, I said, "Hi Cakies! I'm on my way home."

She responded, "Who is this and why are you calling me?" I told her that she was very funny, but once again she said, "No I don't know who you are, and I want to know why you are calling me!" I then asked to speak to Kelsey.

"What is going on with mom?" I asked. Kelsey told me she'd had a fever earlier in the night. Alarms went off inside my brain. I asked what her temperature was and Kelsey told me it was over one hundred. I said, "Get mom dressed. I have to take her to the hospital!" I explained to Kelsey that mom's immune system was down because of the chemotherapy and that we had to be very careful of any infection.

I am usually a slow driver, but after I hung up the phone, I put the pedal to the metal. When I walked in the house, Beth was sitting on the edge of the bed, and Kelsey was trying to get her dressed. Beth was still half asleep from a sleeping pill she'd taken earlier, and she kept trying to get back under the covers. We finally got her dressed and in the car.

We pulled up to the emergency room at the local hospital after midnight. When we finally saw a doctor, he immediately started her on fluids. He gave her an antibiotic through her port to combat the infection. After a couple of hours in a small room with a curtain, I was beginning to grow impatient. It was around 2 a.m. and I was growing weary. I looked at Beth at one point, and she gave me a wink and a smile. I immediately snapped out of my mood and decided to roll with it. Beth was the one who was sick. She was the one who had endured endless treatments and procedures and yet she was able to smile. She never ceased to amaze me. She always managed to find the good in every situation.

After a couple of hours, the emergency room doctor noticed a slight rash on Beth's legs. This was the first time we saw it. She said her legs were a little itchy, but she hadn't thought anything of it. After they finished giving her the antibiotics the doctor said that he was going to let her go home. He made me promise, however, that I would bring her right back in if the fever returned. I promised that I would, and we were on our way home. We finally crawled into bed around five- thirty in the morning.

My alarm went off just before 1 p.m. because I wanted to watch the Michigan Wolverines play BYU in football. Growing up in Michigan, I was a huge fan of the Wolverines. My brother-in-law, George, was somewhat of a father figure to me, and we often watched Michigan football games together. Michigan won 31-0 that day, so I was happy about that.

I hosted a two-hour show from 8 p.m. to 10 p.m. eastern that evening on QVC. When I got home, Beth was fast asleep. I remember kissing her forehead and feeling relieved that she didn't seem to be running a temperature.

The next morning, I took her temperature, and it was normal. She laid down for a nap in the early afternoon and slept until dinner. I cooked steaks that evening, and I thought they turned out perfectly. Because Beth loved steak, I was excited for her to taste it. However, when she woke up, she felt warm to my touch. I took her temperature and it was over 100 degrees. I called Kirstyn and asked her to meet us at the hospital. I needed Kirstyn and Kelsey to stay with her because I was scheduled to host a few hours in prime time that evening on QVC. We checked Beth into the emergency room, and I left the hospital around 6:45 p.m. After my show, I went directly to the hospital. When I walked into the emergency room, I discovered they had just checked her into a room. I stayed with her for about a half-hour. Kirstyn had decided to spend the night with her there, so I went home to sleep.

It was mid-morning when I arrived back at the hospital the next day. I stopped at the gift shop and bought Beth some flowers to brighten up her room. She collected Willow Tree Angels, and I saw one that she didn't have. It was titled *The Angel of Courage*, and it depicted an angel with her arms raised over her head in a V formation. To me, it symbolized that Beth was going to be victorious over cancer. We put it on her nightstand next to her bed in the hospital. I had plenty of faith to believe that she would be healed. There were many times when my faith was tested, but during those times I prayed even harder.

The next day, Kirstyn, Kelsey and I spent most of the day with Beth in her hospital room. That was the day that we met a man that I'll call Dr. Kind (not his real name). He was the doctor assigned to care for Beth. He was a distinguished looking gentleman with a very calm manner about him. He walked into Beth's room with a confident smile. I liked him immediately because he was warm and friendly and he talked to Beth in a very caring and respectful manner.

At one point he turned to me and asked me how I was doing? I told him that I had been talking to the Great Physician about our patient. He smiled and said, "Wonderful because that is who I talk to about all of my patients!" This doctor exuded pure joy. I was so thankful that he was going to care for my Cakies.

Later that afternoon, Beth started saying things that didn't make sense. She suddenly seemed very confused. We thought that it was a reaction to one of the many drugs. As the sun went down, she seemed to be getting worse.

I had to host a show that night at midnight, so I left her room around 9 p.m. to go to the studios. As I walked down the long hallways of the hospital, I began to worry. Beth's health had taken a serious turn for the worse. I prayed all the way to work and all the way through my shift that night. It was so hard to stay cheerful and upbeat when I was on QVC knowing that Beth was literally fighting for her life. Somehow the Lord gave me the strength to get through it.

The next day at the hospital they took some x-rays of Beth's abdominal area and noticed that a couple of her tumors were again pushing on her ureter. They decided to put in two new stints since she was in the hospital. I was with her that entire afternoon. She seemed to be doing all right physically, but her confusion was getting worse. At one point, Kirstyn told me she was concerned that her mom might have suffered a stroke. We talked to Dr. Kind about it, and he said that he felt confident she had not had a stroke, but he ordered a brain scan just to be sure.

I had to head back into work around 8:30 p.m. that night because I was scheduled to be on the air from 11 p.m. until 1 a.m. eastern. Three midnight shifts in a row were challenging when life was normal, but at this point, my stress level was through the roof. The midnight hour sets the tone for the day on QVC so, as a host, I always had an extra run through with the producer, director, and guest before the presentation to make sure we were covering all of the information in a logical, informative and entertaining manner.

Looking back, I realize that it was only by the grace of God that I was able to keep going during this time. I was spending my days in the hospital with Beth and my nights at work. I usually got to bed around 2:30 in the morning and returned to the hospital as soon as I woke up. Kirstyn and Kelsey were also spending a lot of time at the hospital. Kirstyn was busy with work and her family, and Kelsey was working on her master's degree at West Chester University. We were all exhausted and praying for a miracle.

One night I was in the studio getting ready to do a prime-time show. Just a few minutes before my show started, I felt both of my arms go numb. It was a terrifying feeling. I remember trying to shake them out to get the feeling back. For a moment, I thought I was having a heart attack. Suddenly, I felt dizzy, and the studio started spinning on me. I remember looking up at the studio lights, and they appeared to be whirling around above me. It seemed as if the whole studio was on a merry-go-round. I began to pray. I asked God to touch my head, my heart, and my body and to help me make it through the show. He answered my prayer. When the tally light came on, I was calm and focused. The studio stopped spinning and the feeling came back into my arms. It sure felt like a miracle to me!

In the fall of 2015, I needed a miracle every night I was in front of the cameras. I know that many of our QVC viewers were praying for Beth and my family. I want you to know how thankful I am to each and every one of you who prayed for us during this difficult time. Your prayers helped pull us through! This was the biggest challenge of my television career in that I was trying to be positive and full of good energy when I was in front of the cameras all the while knowing that Beth was fighting for her life.

20

A Divine Appointment

The next afternoon Beth's close friend, Sherry Dickey, came to the hospital. Sherry is the type of friend who always wants to help. She had taken Beth to one or two of her chemo treatments and visited her in the hospital. Beth was always happy to see her. Kirstyn, Kelsey and I were also there that day, so Kirstyn suggested that I take a break to get out of the hospital for a while. She told me I should go to the health club and sit in the sauna and just relax. It sounded like a good idea, so I decided to take her up on it.

As you probably know by now, I tend to be a very emotional person. I was trying hard, however, to be strong whenever I was in Beth's hospital room. I didn't want to break down in front of Beth or the girls. I was doing pretty well up to this point, but as I walked toward the elevators that afternoon, my emotions began to well up inside of me. When the elevator doors opened, I was relieved to see that it was empty. I stepped in, and as soon as the doors closed, I bent over and started to weep. When the doors opened on the first floor, I was still crying. I got off the elevator and leaned against a wall and just put my head in my hands.

Suddenly I heard a voice calling, "Mr. Wheeler! What is the matter?" I looked up and saw Dr. Kind jogging toward me.

He came up and gave me a big hug (something very rare for a medical doctor to do in a hospital).

I looked at him and said, "Dr. Kind, this is overwhelming. My wife has been fighting stage 4 Cancer for almost three years, and now we are in a tough stage. I'm worried, and I need a miracle. I just hope that God hears my prayers."

I'll never forget what he said to me. He looked me squarely in the eye and said, "Mr. Wheeler because you want to know if God hears your prayers, I will tell you what just happened to me. I finished eating my lunch in the cafeteria a few minutes ago. I was hurrying to go up to the second floor to make my rounds because I have several patients that I need to check on, and I try never to be late. As I arrived right here to get on this elevator, something told me to go back to the cafeteria. I walked all the way back, and when I got there I thought to myself, why did I come back here? I need to get to my patients. As I started walking back, I saw you get off the elevator, and I knew why I was delayed. God cares enough about you to change my schedule so that I was right here right now to tell you that He cares about you very much. He hears every one of your prayers, and He knows what is going on."

He then said, "Mr. Wheeler I know this is extremely difficult for you and your family. However, your wife knows Jesus, and you know where she is going if she doesn't survive. God can heal her here on earth, or he can give her a new body in heaven. Either way, she will be healed, and you will see her again." He gave me another hug and then got on the elevator.

As I walked out of the hospital, I realized that God had just performed a miracle. He delayed Dr. Kind enough so that he could be there when I needed to be reminded that God loved us, and He was still with us.

Some people might call that meeting a coincidence. I believe that God delayed Dr. Kind. It is highly unusual for a medical doctor to hug and encourage a family member in the hallway of a hospital. It doesn't happen every day, but it happened on the day that I needed it. I believe it was a divine appointment. It was the first of several miracles I would see during the next thirty days.

Beth had a brain scan the next day, and it confirmed what Dr. Kind thought. She had not suffered a stroke. Her brain was fine. I was with her when they did the scan. As we were waiting, I leaned down, kissed her and told her how much I loved her. She then asked me to lean back down because she wanted to say something. She whispered in my ear, "Cakies, you need some breath mints because you have really bad breath." We both had a good laugh from that, and I was happy to see that Beth hadn't lost her sense of humor through it all.

21

A Cardinal Visit

I don't remember anything specific about that weekend in the hospital, but I do remember it was nice just to be with Beth and our daughters. Our family was together, and that is what mattered. Hospitals are always quieter on weekends because there are not as many doctors making their rounds. We all just hung out together in Beth's room, and enjoyed being together.

Beth always expressed her appreciation to every person who came in her room, whether it was a member of the cleaning staff or a doctor. The nurses all told us that she was their favorite patient. They said they came in early each day to request her as their patient.

By Monday, October 5th, Beth seemed to be less confused. She wasn't saying as many bizarre things. It seemed like she'd been on a four-day vacation and was coming home. Kirstyn and I took turns staying with her at night because we wanted to make sure that she was getting the proper care.

Beth was in a great hospital, but mistakes happen even at the best. Kirstyn knew that first-hand from her nursing experience. She told us that one of us needed to be there with her at all times.

When Kirstyn spent the night, I came home and wrote Beth

a good night text. I told her how much I loved her and that I was hoping she would come back to us soon. When we were concerned about her mental state, she wasn't able to answer. I'll never forget how excited I was when she finally answered me back and told me she loved me.

I was getting out of bed early in the morning on Tuesday, October 6th when I received a call from Kirstyn. There was a sense of urgency in her voice as she said, "Dad, you need to get here as quickly as you can!"

"What's going on?" I asked. She told me that Beth's platelet count had dropped to 3,000. She explained that a normal platelet count for a healthy person is somewhere between 150,000 and 400,000 per microliter of circulating blood. At 3,000 per microliter, Beth's platelets were dangerously low. I told her I would be right there.

I had to take Zoey outside before I left for the day. As I walked into the kitchen to get her, I looked at our empty bird feeder outside the window. We usually kept it full of birdseed because we loved seeing the birds up close. Our favorite bird was the male cardinal because my mom always said that whenever she saw a male cardinal, she believed it was God's sign that everything was going to be ok. Beth and I adapted that belief, but I hadn't seen a male cardinal for a long time. On this morning, I whispered a prayer and said something like this, "Dear Lord. I could use a sign that everything is going to be ok. I would love to see a red cardinal." I hadn't seen one in at least five or six weeks, and since we didn't have any birdseed in the feeder, I honestly did not expect to see one.

I took Zoey outside, and when she finished, I ran inside and threw my clothes on. As I walked into the kitchen on my way to the garage, I looked at the empty bird feeder. Almost as if on cue, a bright red male cardinal flew up, landed on the bird feeder and looked at me. I couldn't believe my eyes! I said, "Thank you, Lord Jesus! I really needed to see him today!"

On my way to the hospital, I called my sister, Margie Lou. She is a prayer warrior, and when she answered, I said, "Margie, Beth needs your prayers right now. Her platelets are dangerously low, and we need a miracle!" She prayed the most beautiful prayer. Tears streamed down my face as I prayed along with her. That morning the Holy Spirit took over. I felt His presence in a powerful way.

When I walked into Beth's room, the nurses were already starting to give her a bag of platelets. They told me it would give her platelet count a big boost. It didn't work. After they gave her the platelets, her count plunged to 2,300. The nurses and doctors seemed to go into emergency mode at this point. Dr. Kind was on the phone with Dr. Gale in Philadelphia. She said that she wanted Beth to be transferred to the hospital downtown so she could monitor her more closely. This is the same hospital where Beth had her surgery almost three years earlier. It felt like we were in a major crisis. I saw worry and concern on the faces of the nurses and the doctors.

It turned out to be a very long day as we waited for the logistics of the transfer to be worked out. I decided that I was going to follow the ambulance and stay with Beth at the hospital in Philadelphia. Kirstyn had to go home to be with her kids. Her husband, Jeff, was accommodating and understanding. He was juggling his work schedule to give Kirstyn as much time as possible to be with her mom. By this point, her kids were missing her, and the downtown hospital was over an hour away.

Beth slept on and off most of that day while I waited and prayed. Thankfully, I had some unexpected visitors. My boss, Jack Comstock, and Caroline Stueck, a director in our department, came by to offer their love and support. I had told Jack about Beth's comment to me over the weekend that I needed breath mints. He brought me a nice card and a bag filled with Tic-Tac breath mints. I needed some comic relief at this point, so we all had a good laugh. It was great to see them, and even though Beth spent most of the afternoon resting, they were able to visit with her for a few minutes. Another great friend, Steve Long, came by. Ironically, Steve's first wife had passed away from cancer several years earlier on the same floor of the same hospital.

Their visit was perfectly timed. I told them that I would be following Beth down to Philadelphia and that I had no idea what was ahead. Jack and Caroline told me not to worry about work. The entire host team stepped up to fill in for me. I will be forever grateful to them for giving me the precious gift of time with Beth. Unfortunately, time was running out.

Our dear friends, Russ and Trish Whitnah, came by about an hour after the others left. Beth perked up when she saw them. We were in a Bible Study with them when we first moved to Pennsylvania. Kirstyn played soccer with their daughter, Sara, in elementary school and middle school. We always enjoyed spending time with them. Trish was another person who considered Beth to be one of her very best friends and Beth felt the same way about her.

I know that having a seriously ill friend in the hospital can feel awkward when you visit. You may wonder what you will say and whether your words will make any difference. Let me assure you: for the patient, and the family, your presence says more than your words. You don't have to worry about what to say. When you are simply there, praying for and loving your sick friend, you do make a difference. The people who were there for Beth and me made these days easier than they ever would have been if we had been alone.

22

The Scariest Drive of My Life

It was a long day, and it would have been even longer if friends hadn't stopped by the hospital. I knew the plan was to transport Beth to the downtown hospital, but I didn't know exactly when that was going to happen.

Dr. Kind had explained to me that Dr. Gale wanted Beth to be downtown, not only to monitor her more closely, but also to have access to platelets that were more closely matched to hers. He explained that the other hospital was equipped to handle the delivery of HLA matched platelets. That was the first time I heard that term. I knew that platelets helped our blood to clot. Without platelets, we would bleed to death every time we got a cut. But I had never heard about HLA- matched platelets.

I discovered that the Red Cross has an impressive computer system that scours blood banks around the country to find as close to an exact match of a person's platelets as possible. When Beth received the normal bag of platelets, her body thought they were a foreign substance, so her blood attacked the platelets and chewed them up. She would have a better chance of accepting the HLA-matched platelets because they would be almost identical to hers. (HLA stands for Human Leukocyte Antigen— leukocytes are white blood cells, and antigens, of course, are toxins that trigger the immune system; basically HLA- matched platelets have fewer antigens to the specific patient's system, so they're more likely to be accepted in the bloodstream.)

It takes a while for hospitals to coordinate the transport of a patient with the ambulance company. They have to make sure the ambulance and personnel are equipped to handle any possible complications the patient might encounter *en route*. My wait time that day seemed like an eternity.

Word finally came that they were coming to pick up Beth around eight o'clock in the evening. Since it was already six o'clock, I decided I had better quickly drive home and pack a suitcase, because I was planning to stay with Beth in Philly. I had no idea how long I would be there. I quickly packed up her room and filled a couple of boxes with flowers, photos and knick-knacks we had brought in to make her room feel more like home.

I made it back to the hospital around seven- thirty. I had a nice long talk with Beth, explaining what was happening. I assured her that I would be driving down to Philly to stay with her in the hospital. When the transport people came to her room, the entire staff on that floor lined the hallway to say their goodbyes to Beth and wish her well. Many were crying as they told her how much they would miss her. Their outpouring of love deeply moved me. My eyes welled up with tears as I watched them hug her. You could tell they all cared about her. She had only been a patient there for eight days, yet they all fell in love with her. It was impossible not to, because of the way she loved everyone she came in contact with. No matter how badly she felt she was kind, thankful and appreciative to every person who helped her and she always told them so. It was another example of how her hurricane of love hit everyone in its path!

As soon as the transport people put Beth on the elevator, I finished packing up the last of her belongings and headed to my car. As I pulled out of the parking lot, I felt a wave of fear come over me. I wondered what was around this next turn on our journey. Beth's health was rapidly deteriorating. I did my best to keep my mind on the Lord. I thought of one of my favorite verses in the Bible, **Isaiah 26:3.** It says, **"Thou dost keep him in perfect peace whose mind is stayed on thee because he trusts in thee."-King James Version of the Bible.** I did my best to keep my mind on the Lord to keep the fear from gripping me any further.

I called Kirstyn and told her that I was scared. I will never forget what she said to me. "Dad, you've got this! You have turned into an excellent nurse. You know what to watch for, and you know what questions to ask the doctors. I will be down in a day or two, but you can call me anytime." It reminded me of a pep talk that I used to give to her before one of her lacrosse games, and here she was giving me one at this critical juncture in our lives. Then she further encouraged me by saying, "Dad, a few years ago, I would never have believed that you could do what you have been doing. But you are doing a great job of taking care of mom. You are going to be okay. Have faith and remember you can handle this!" She gave me a renewed sense of confidence.

Kirstyn & Beth on Kirstyn's wedding day-September 5, 2010.

As I drove on towards Philadelphia, the night seemed extra dark, and the road felt extra lonely. I thought about my conversation with Kirstyn, and I decided it was time for a major conversation with God. I told Him that I was scared and that I needed His wisdom in the days ahead. "I don't know what the future holds but I know that you hold the future. Please give me the strength that I need; give Beth peace, comfort, and healing, and please give the doctors wisdom as they treat her. Thank you, Lord Jesus, that you are with us on this journey," I prayed. I immediately felt a deep sense of peace come over me.

When I walked into Beth's room in the Philadelphia hospital, two nurses were getting ready to clean her up. It was cold in the room, and she hardly had anything on. The nurses were taking their good old sweet time and seemed oblivious to the fact that Beth was freezing. The goose bumps all over her body were a pretty good clue not to mention the fact that she was shaking.

Interrupting their conversation about their social life, I told them their patient was cold, and I politely asked if they could get her a blanket. Beth gave me a look that said, "Don't rock the boat." I knew that look very well.

One of the nurses said something like, "It's ok pops, we know what we're doing and we've got it under control."

Because I didn't want to say something I would regret, I bit my lip and went straight to the nursing station. I announced that I needed to speak to the charge nurse right away. She was actually at the desk and walked out into the hall and asked me what was wrong. I told her that my wife was freezing while the two nurses who were giving her a sponge bath were taking their time and letting her shiver. I then informed her that my wife's platelets were extremely low and that she deserved better treatment. "I want someone in there who will treat my wife with the respect and care she deserves, and I don't ever want to see those two nurses in her room again!", I stated emphatically.

I couldn't just let this slide. Beth was in a fight for her life, and I wasn't going to put up with that kind of treatment at a hospital that was renowned for their excellence in care. The charge nurse went straight to Beth's room and told the nurses they were being reassigned. She then brought in two nurses who were incredibly kind, and we never saw the other two again.

I know that nurses have a very tough job. I know it first-hand because Kirstyn is a nurse and a very good one (yes, I'm partial because she's my daughter, but I've heard this from several doctors and nurses who have worked with her). She always puts her patients first. She has told me how some patients are extremely difficult, and that it is tough to care for someone who is unappreciative. Beth, however, was always very appreciative of everything. Kirstyn said that she had never had a patient that was as sweet, kind and appreciative as her mom. That is why the attitudes of the first two nurses that night were so upsetting to me. I was going to make sure Beth got the respect and the care that she deserved all the time.

Before Beth fell asleep that night, a nurse came in with a bag of platelets. I remember she said, "We have to give her this bag of regular platelets before we can get the HLA- matched platelets. This is procedural. We know that these platelets won't work." She then inserted a tube from the bag into Beth's port and hung the bag of platelets on the hook at the top of the pole by her bed.

When she left the room, I walked up to the bag of platelets and put my hands on it. I asked God to cause those platelets to work. "Lord please let these platelets work. You made Beth's platelets, and you can surely work through these! Please help her platelet level to rise. Amen."

The night was long, and my sleeping hours were short. I have always wondered how anyone can rest in a hospital. The nurses come in every couple hours to take the patient's vital signs, change the bag of fluids, draw blood, etc. There was a chair in Beth's room that supposedly converted to a bed. It was more like a series of three narrow boxes in a row. The sheets kept falling off every time I moved. I knew sleep would be just a dream, so I tossed and turned and prayed all night long.

The next morning another nurse came in to take Beth's vitals and draw her blood. They constantly monitored the critical aspects of her blood including her platelets, red blood cells, white blood cells, and plasma. I asked when they would have the results from her recent blood work because I was curious as to whether her platelet count changed from the bag of regular platelets. She told me they would have it in about a half hour. It seemed like she returned an hour later but she informed me Beth's platelets were at forty- three. I asked her if she meant 4300 and she said yes. I was hoping for a higher number, but I was encouraged that her platelets went from 2300 to 4300 per microliter. I thought: at least she is moving in the right direction.

Later that morning, I was introduced to Beth's team of

hematologists. One of the reasons this hospital is renowned for the quality of care is that a patient is assigned a team of doctors for every major medical issue the patient has. During this meeting, I asked the head doctor what he thought about Beth's platelets going from 2300 to 4300 after they gave her the bag of regular platelets. He looked at me and said her platelets went from 2300 to 43,000, not 4300. I'll never forget the surge of hope that ran through me at that moment. I said, "Praise the Lord! Hallelujah! We are going in the right direction!" They all agreed that was a big jump, considering the fact that the day before her platelets *dropped* after she was given a regular bag of platelets.

This was the beginning of a two-week emotional roller coaster ride for my family. Every morning and every afternoon after they drew a blood sample we waited anxiously for the results. By late afternoon that first day, Beth's platelet count had fallen back down to 20,000. The next morning her count was down to 11,000, and by afternoon it was in dangerous territory again at 8,000. Our hope turned to the HLA- matched platelets. The only problem was, they hadn't come in yet.

During our second night in this hospital, a phlebotomist came into Beth's room shortly after midnight and announced that he was there to draw some blood. It was dark, and I was in my "bed," so I stayed there to let the man do his job, which was fairly routine: Beth's blood was easily drawn through her port. Because she had low platelets, it would be dangerous to draw blood using a needle—low platelets mean blood can't coagulate as it should, and there's the chance bleeding can't be stopped, so needles aren't used at all.

After the phlebotomist left, Beth needed to use the restroom, so I got up to help her out of bed—and felt that her arm was wet as I touched her. I turned on the light and was horrified to see blood running down her arm! I immediately ran out to the front desk and told a nurse what had happened. She was extremely upset, as it stated very clearly on Beth's chart that she was not to be stuck with a needle. Apparently, the phlebotomist misread or just missed the instruction on her chart. I didn't sleep at all that night because I was worried about the possibility of Beth bleeding uncontrollably due to her low platelet count.

The next morning the nurse checked her arm, and miraculously her blood clotted to the point where the bleeding stopped. They kept a tight bandage on it as a precautionary measure.

Later that afternoon, I went down to the hospital's main lobby to stretch my legs and get a change of scenery while Beth took her afternoon nap. A woman approached me and asked if I was Dan Wheeler. I said I was, and she introduced herself and told me that she had watched me on television for many years. As it turned out, she was the head of patient safety at the hospital. She then handed me her card and said to notify her if I needed anything while Beth was in the hospital. I said, "You are just the person I need to talk to!"

When I told her what had happened to Beth the night before, she was appalled. After apologizing profusely, she promised she would get to the bottom of it. I told her I wasn't angry, and I didn't want anyone to get fired, but I was very concerned that this had happened and I didn't want it to happen again to any other patient.

Remember, it is important to have a close friend or family member with your loved one at all times if they are hospitalized with a serious health issue. They need an advocate!

After two days of watching Beth's platelet count go up and down, we were excited when her HLA- matched platelets arrived. She received the first bag, and her count soared from 11,000 to 41,000. I was a little disappointed, because I thought the matched platelets would bring her back up to a normal level of 150,000 or more. However, when Dr. Gale stopped by

Beth's room that night, she told us she was very pleased with that number. She explained that the goal was to get Beth's bone marrow to fire back up to where she was producing her own platelets again. She told us this number represented a good start. We had to hope that Beth's body would accept and hang onto these new platelets until her bone marrow started working properly again.

I walked Dr. Gale out of the hospital that night. It was late and as I said good night, she turned to me and said, "Dan, when a woman your wife's age comes into our practice with the type of cancer that your wife has, we usually give her a year to live at the most. Your wife has made it three years. And I want you to know that is a miracle." She went on to say that our family had made a tremendous impact on the entire hospital. She told me that Beth's reputation as a kind, sweet, and loving patient had spread to all the doctors and nurses. "Everyone is talking about that wonderful lady and her caring and supportive family. It is a rare thing to find such kindness at a time of such great crisis like you are experiencing," she said.

I told her that we were stressed out like everyone else at the hospital and that we were leaning on the Lord to help us through. I also said how much we appreciated her care and her love for Beth.

As I walked back up to Beth's room, I thanked God for giving us this skillful and knowledgeable doctor. And I thanked Him for Beth's beautiful example of grace, strength, and love in the face of a life-threatening illness. I fell asleep that night replaying everything Dr. Gale had said. I knew that she was appreciative of our attitude and our perseverance. I also felt that she was letting me know that the end of our journey might be quickly approaching.

I had learned my way around Beth's floor reasonably well by this time. Sometimes when she was asleep, I walked down the hallway to say hello to the other patients. There was a sweet, elderly woman in the room next to Beth's who was always alone whenever I walked by. I felt bad for her, so I tried to stop in and chat with her whenever Beth was sleeping. I remember one day I asked if I could pray for her. A big smile came across her face, and she said that she would greatly appreciate prayer. After I prayed for her, she told me she felt a sense of peace come over her.

Beth's brother, Roy Johnson, drove out from Chicago around this time. He had stayed in close contact with me throughout Beth's hospitalization and relayed information to her side of the family. Roy was growing concerned over the way things were going, and he told me he wanted to come out and see his sister and help in any way he could. I told him that I would greatly appreciate it if he could come and help us.

He was indeed a huge help! He stayed at our house with Kelsey and took care of Zoey. He also cooked several meals for us. Kelsey was living at home while working on her master's degree. She was often alone for long periods of time while Beth and I were at the hospital in Philadelphia. I had been worried about Kelsey, and I was happy that she would have uncle Roy in the house with her. I was glad to have someone to confide in about my concerns over Beth's health. Roy's presence was a blessing. He took a load off my mind. He came down to the hospital and spent some time with Beth during the week, and his visits gave her spirits a boost.

Kirstyn was busy at home with her two young boys at the time, but she offered to come down to give me a break on Friday night. Since Jeff was going to be home on the weekend, he was able to watch Cole and Gavin. This was her best chance to come down and be with her mom, and it allowed me a night to recharge my batteries by sleeping in my own bed. I remember that I was also thrilled to be able to take my first shower of the week.

On the drive home, I called my good friend, Dr. John

Cooke. John is an internist who was practicing in Florida. I had contacted him on a couple of occasions over the years when family members were facing health issues. He always had a knack for correctly diagnosing things over the phone, even when other doctors struggled. When I told him what was going on with Beth, he told me it was outside of his area of expertise. But he said he knew a doctor who would know exactly what was happening. His daughter, Sara, specialized in oncological hematology, the study of blood in cancer patients. He said he would get ahold of her and have her call me as soon as possible.

Within fifteen minutes, Sara called and explained that what was going on with Beth was something called Idiopathic Thrombocytopenia Purpura or ITP. She said that the many chemotherapy treatments had severely weakened Beth's bone marrow to the point that it could no longer produce platelets. I told her that the doctors were trying the HLA- matched platelets. She assured me that was the right course of action and said that hopefully her bone marrow would eventually fire back up and produce platelets on its own. This was exactly what Dr. Gale had told me.

As I arrived home, I thanked her for calling me back and giving me the information. It is always good to have the opinion of a specialist when you or a loved one is facing a serious health issue. This was beyond serious.

After sleeping for nine hours, I woke up and immediately called Kirstyn. She told me Beth's platelet count had fallen slightly but that she was encouraged that it had held better with the HLA- matched platelets than it did with the regular ones. Our emotional roller coaster was once again at a high point. But I knew it could be headed back down at any moment.

It was early afternoon when I made it back to Beth's room. We spent a relatively quiet weekend together, and Beth was finally able to get some meaningful rest.

I'd decided to get a room at a hotel close to the hospital, so

I could at least sleep in a bed at night. I'd found a nice hotel nearby that offered hourly shuttles to and from the hospital. This allowed me to leave my car in the hospital parking garage and shuttle back and forth. I tried to catch the earliest shuttle to the hospital every day at seven in the morning and the last one back to the hotel at ten o'clock every night.

I could tell Beth was getting weaker by the day, but she continued to keep her spirits high. The rash on her legs had become much worse. It was dark purple, and it now covered both of her legs and even started to move up into her abdominal area. She was having a difficult time controlling her bodily functions. She wasn't comfortable having the nurses help her go to the bathroom. She was the most comfortable with either Kirstyn or me. We were both glad to be able to help her. Kirstyn taught me the best way to get her up and into the bathroom. When she had to go, I immediately unplugged her I.V., wrapped it around the stand and swung her legs over the edge of the bed. I learned how to pull her up onto her feet by grabbing the back of both of her arms by her triceps as she grabbed onto my forearms. We counted one, two three and lifted her onto her feet. After she finished in the bathroom, I would go in, clean her up and then walk her back to bed and plug her I.V. back in. Most days we did this between six to eight times and once in a while even more.

I went a little overboard in my enthusiasm while caring for Beth. No matter what she wanted or needed, I always jumped up and tried to get it for her right away. Kirstyn loved to imitate me. She always made us laugh when she would say, "Here is Dad: *What? Beth needs the nurse?*" and she would run out of the room like a crazy person who was going to tackle a nurse. She provided some much needed comic relief.

One day as I was helping Beth back to bed she looked at me and said, "Cakies, what would I ever do without you?"

I said, "You will never need to know! I will always be here

for you." It felt so good to be able to say that and absolutely mean it.

I was exhausted and running on nervous energy. The platelet count readings had me on an emotional roller coaster. I remember many times I would fall into the recliner next to Beth's bed after a bathroom visit. I would look up and whisper, "Lord I don't have anything left." In His still small voice, I felt like God was saying, "Good. Now I can work because when you are weak, I am strong. Remember I am the source of your strength."

One night early on during Beth's stay in the Philly Hospital, a nurse came in late in the evening to check on Beth. Before she left the room, she entered some information into a computer screen that was attached to the wall. After she walked out of the room, the computer screen stayed on, and it was shining directly onto Beth's face. After waiting for about a minute (it seemed like ten), I got up and walked over to the screen. I noticed there was a lever on the side and I thought I could darken the screen if I pulled it down. As soon as I did several loud alarms went off. I stepped out into the hallway, and all of the nurses and doctors on the floor were running toward me as fast as they could! I put up my arms and waved at them and said, "I'm so sorry! I pulled that lever! It was an accident." They all stopped in their tracks. None of them thought it was funny. I had pulled the lever to signal Code Blue! It was definitely one of the most embarrassing moments of my life.

When I look back now, I realize what an honor it was to help care for Beth. She would have done it for me a thousand times over. I remember looking at her swollen hands and thinking that those hands had prepared thousands of meals for our family; did thousands of loads of laundry; took care of our daughters when they were babies and little girls; painted and wall-papered the walls of our homes; they had touched many sad faces and wiped away the tears; they gave the best hugs and said "I love you" in so many ways. I thank God that I was able to be there with her every step of this journey. Caring for her was truly a privilege.

I taped photographs of our family on the wall directly in front of Beth's bed at eye level. There were pictures of Kirstyn and Kelsey when they were little girls, and there were pictures of Beth and me when we were in our twenties and thirties. I brought in photos of many other family members as well. We looked at those photographs every day and reminisced about each one. I tried to use them to motivate her to keep fighting. I reminded her how important she was to every person in every picture. I told her that we were all looking forward to many more happy times with her.

My coworkers on the QVC host team continued to be amazingly supportive. One day, fellow host Courtney Cason came to the hospital with several bags of personal care products for Beth. She also brought us food from a fabulous Italian caterer, because she knew we were growing tired of the hospital fare. Shawn Killinger sent me a text one day telling me she was praying for Beth, my entire family and me. She wrote, "My dear friend Dan. You are truly playing in the big leagues of life right now. I know this is the toughest time of your life, but I also know that your faith in God will pull you through. Love, Shawn." My great friends and fellow QVC hosts Rick Domeier and Mary Beth Roe brought us home-cooked meals. Nancy Hornback, Pat James-Dementri, Dan Hughes, Jane Treacy, Sandra Bennett, Sharon Faetsch, Jill Bauer, David Venable and the entire host team (there are too many to list them all), along with others, reached out to me with words of support during this time. My good friend, Tom Czar and his wife Denise, came by the house several times to drop off food for our family.

I learned that when someone is going through a trying time, it is best to just show up and help. People always say, "Let me know if there is anything I can do to help." Well, the fact is you are so occupied that you don't think about

asking others for help because it is so hard to even think of how they can help. Just show up with food, an encouraging word, a comforting hug or all three! Also, please give blood including platelets if you are able. I am thankful to the people who donated the platelets that kept Beth alive. Since I have a rare blood type I try to donate whenever I can. Your blood and platelets can save a life!

One night I arrived back to the hotel very late in the evening. As I slipped into bed, my phone rang. It was my friend, Dr. John Cooke, from Florida. He asked me how I was doing and then he said, "Dan, as your friend, I have to tell you that Beth is probably not going to make it through this unless God performs a miracle." I told him I knew. "I just got off the phone with my daughter, Sara, and she told me that I needed to let you know as your friend. Since the HLA- matched platelets haven't been holding her levels there is very little chance she will survive," he continued. I waited and then asked him if he had ever seen a medical miracle. He said, "Yes!"

"Well, I am hanging onto the hope that God will perform a miracle, so I am not ready to let my mind go anywhere else," I said. He told me that was the best thing to do. I hung up the phone and dropped to my knees by the bed. I told the Lord that I knew He could perform a miracle and completely heal Beth. I then asked Him to do just that. Then I added, "Not my will but yours be done."

The next day I met with all of Beth's doctors. The head of her hematology team told me the HLA-matched platelets weren't doing the job, and they were running out of options. He looked at me and said, "What is the goal at this point?"

I immediately responded, "To bring her home. I don't want her dying in a hospital." He told me that was a wise goal, and he and the other teams of doctors started putting things in place for Beth to be released.

During one of my other meetings that day I had a doctor tell me they wanted to test Beth's bone marrow. I asked him how he planned on doing that. He told me they wanted to collect a sample of her tissue from her hip. I looked at him and said, "Will this help you cure my wife?" He fumbled for his words and said something like he wasn't sure but that it would give them information. I very emphatically said, "NO! My wife is NOT a medical experiment. I've heard that is an excruciating procedure and unless you can tell me with no uncertainty that it will help you cure her then I won't even consider it!" I was angry, and he knew it. He apologized, and that was the end of that discussion.

On Thursday a young social worker walked into Beth's room and told me they were going to discharge her the next day. I was taken by surprise and said that we weren't ready. We had to talk about the medical equipment that was needed; it had to be ordered and delivered to the house. We hadn't discussed how Beth would receive the HLA-matched platelets that were keeping her alive, and I didn't even know how we would get Beth in and out of the house for those treatments. She agreed that there was too much to be done, so we decided to aim to bring her home the following Tuesday, October 20th.

In meeting with Dr. Gale and her team later that day, she suggested that arrangements be made for Beth to receive her platelets at a facility in Valley Forge which was a half hour closer to our home. I said that would be great but how would we get her there? Dr. Gale said she would make arrangements for an ambulance to take her. Dr. Gale had so much love and compassion for Beth, and she wanted to try everything possible to keep her alive.

Thursday and Friday of that week we made our plans with the direction of the doctors and the social worker. By the time Friday night rolled around we were ready to rest.

One of our dear friends, Kendy Walor, was in town and asked if she could visit Beth on Friday. Beth was happy when I told her! Kendy was my co-host on the first home shopping show I hosted in Chicago in 1986. Kendy, Jane Lynch (yes *that* Jane Lynch, television and movie star) and I were the hosts of a show called *America's Shopping Place*. The show was produced five nights a week out of Telemation studios in Glenview, Illinois.

I was the co-owner of a production company in Chicago called Closer Look Video Group at the time, so when the shopping show ended, I continued to work at Closer Look. Kendy, however, landed a job as a host on the Cable Value Network (CVN) in Plymouth, Minnesota. Jane took off for Hollywood and obviously has enjoyed a very successful career.

CVN eventually came after me because they had seen me on Kendy's audition reel. I didn't know other shopping networks existed at the time. I thought home shopping was a fad that probably wouldn't last (little did I know!) HSN (Home Shopping Network) and CVN eventually pursued me. I liked CVN but didn't seriously consider leaving the company I had started with my good friend, Dave Ormesher. However, my phone kept ringing. A guy named Bob Sanders from CVN called me every Friday with a slightly higher offer. Finally, the offer became too good to pass up. It was hard to part with Dave, but I felt it was the right move for my family. Beth, our three-year-old daughter, Kirstyn, and I moved to Minnesota where I worked with Kendy.

After a couple of months at CVN, I began hosting the noon to 3 p.m. slot on Monday through Friday, which allowed me to enjoy lots of quality time with my family. Kirstyn was just a little girl, and I was able to be home with her and Beth in the evenings and on weekends. Life was terrific in Minnesota—until the day we were told that QVC was buying CVN and most of us would be losing our jobs.

QVC was very good to all of us who weren't offered jobs. QVC took four female hosts but none of the guys. They gave us very generous severance packages. I had only been there for a year and three months before we moved back to Chicago. I went to work for a friend of mine named Don Hancock at his production company, producing mainly corporate videos once again. About a year later, QVC came calling, and we moved to the West Chester, Pennsylvania area. Kendy joined QVC a couple of years later, but only stayed for a year. I stayed for twenty- nine years. However, Kendy and I always remained close friends.

At this time, October of 2015, Kendy's daughter, Tru, had started her freshman year at a college in Philadelphia. Kendy was in town helping her get settled and had a couple of free nights, so she came to see Beth in the hospital on Friday, October 16. We had a wonderful time reminiscing about fun times together in Illinois, Minnesota, and Pennsylvania. Kendy lifted Beth's spirits. After a few hours, as she was getting ready to leave, she asked if she could come back on Saturday. We said, "Of course!"

Michigan was playing their in-state rival, Michigan State, in football on Saturday so I had the game on in Beth's room when Kendy came back. Michigan had the game won with just seconds to go and a narrow lead. All they had to do was punt the ball away and hold the Spartans on one down. However, the Michigan punter fumbled the snap, and Michigan State recovered it and scored a touchdown as time expired to win the game. I was devastated—and I was glad Kendy was there to cheer me up.

As she hugged Beth goodbye, she had tears in her eyes. When I walked her to the elevator, we both broke down and cried. We realized it was probably the last time that Kendy would see Beth alive.

23

*W*elcome Home Beth

Beth was very close with her brother, Roy, and her sister, Carol Bellone. Carol lived south of San Francisco at the time. Roy kept Carol up to date on Beth's health, and she decided that it was time to come and spend some time with her sister. She flew out on Sunday, October 18th. We decided we were going to surprise Beth, so we didn't tell her she was coming. Roy picked her up at the airport and brought her straight to the hospital.

As I mentioned earlier, Beth was always hard to surprise, but I loved it when we pulled it off, and this was one of those times. Roy texted me when they were inside the hospital on their way up to the room. My heart started beating faster as I awaited their arrival. Beth loved Carol, and I knew she would be so happy to see her. They called each other see-ster, and Beth always said, "I love my sees-ter so much!" Roy walked in and apologized for being late. He told Beth that he had been out shopping for a "welcome home" present for her. He said he found the perfect present and he didn't want to wait until Tuesday to give it to her. He said that he left it in the hall, so he walked out and then brought Carol back in and said, "Here is your present!" Beth was shocked and soooo happy to see Carol. They gave each other major hugs and kisses.

Beth, Carol, and Roy had a sweet little family reunion. There was a lot of reminiscing and plenty of laughter. Beth eventually grew tired and was starting to fall asleep as we said goodnight and left her room. We were all very hungry, so we stopped for some food on the way home. Roy and Carol were happy to see each other, but they wished it were under better circumstances. I did too.

Beth, her brother Roy and her sister Carol- circa 2007.

The next day we hit the ground running. As I was getting ready to drive back to the hospital, I called my good friend, Bryan Law. Bryan is a highly skilled carpenter and builder. When he answered the phone, I asked, "Bryan do you know how to build a ramp for someone in a wheelchair?" I explained to him that we were bringing Beth home from the hospital the next day and asked if there was any way he could build the ramp by the end of the week.

He said, "I'll come over and build it today! I will move my other jobs back, so you will have it ready when she comes home tomorrow!" As I hung up, I thanked the Lord for giving me such a loyal friend. He dropped everything to help us out. I will always be grateful for his friendship and his demonstration of love for us.

Carol and I were on the road back to the hospital by 8:30 that morning. She had a notepad and a pen, and we started making a list of all the things we needed to get done that day to bring Beth home. There were dozens of details that had to be worked out. I called Dr. Gale from the car, and she told me her team was working on all the details of in-home visits, platelet transfusions, transportation, etc. We called the medical equipment company to order the hospital equipment to be delivered to the house by the next day. When we arrived at the hospital, we had a long meeting with the social worker and made sure all of the bases were covered for Beth's departure the next day. As if that weren't enough, we also had our final meetings with Beth's three teams of doctors.

We finally returned home late in the afternoon and, to my surprise, Bryan was almost finished building the ramp from our driveway up to the front door. He told me he would come back the next morning to finish it up well in advance of Beth's arrival home. I was scheduled to host that evening's midnight show on QVC, so I tried to take a quick nap. I had so much on my mind that I couldn't sleep. Since I had already missed a couple of weeks of work, I wanted to host as many shows as I could, while I could.

The fact that Beth was coming home after three weeks in the hospital had me feeling better as I drove into QVC Studio Park that evening. My product lineup that night featured a lot of holiday décor items. I made it through my show prep and the rehearsal without a problem. In the middle of my show, however, the thought popped into my mind that Beth might not be here for Christmas. I never knew when things like that would hit me while I was in front of the cameras. I tried so hard to focus on what I was doing, but every once in a while those thoughts came out of the blue. As you can imagine, it was challenging trying to be cheerful in front of the cameras. It took every ounce of energy and discipline I could find.

As promised, Bryan was back working on the ramp early the next morning. By the time I woke up around 10 a.m. he was putting on the finishing touches. I thanked him for coming over and building it so quickly, and I gave him a check that he was hesitant to accept. I was so appreciative of the fact that he dropped everything and made our ramp a priority.

Later in the day, I walked into the kitchen, and I found my dear, sweet friend Mary Beth Roe filling my refrigerator with food. She said she knew I had a lot of people over and probably wouldn't have time to go to the grocery store. A few weeks earlier, my buddy, Rick Domeier had showed up with lots of delicious food that his wife, Amy, had made for us. These are examples of love in action. **(Remember just *show up* when a friend or loved one is in need. They are probably too overwhelmed to ask for your help so just show up—and bring food!)**

Our house was bustling with activity. The medical supply company delivered the wheelchair, bedside commode, walker and a hospital bed. Our neighbor, Dana Poirier, came by with a big homemade "Welcome Home Beth" sign. I hung it up in the bedroom directly in front of where Beth would be lying in bed. Our neighbors Bill and Diane Riley brought over "Welcome Home" balloons and decorations. It was a happy day.

Kirstyn drove to the hospital to help check Beth out. She called us when they took Beth out of her room to be transported. She told me that the nurses, assistants, and doctors once again lined the hall to hug Beth and wish her well. There were lots of tears as they all said their goodbyes. Kirstyn said she was amazed at the impact her mom had made. Beth's love left its imprint on the heart of every person she came in contact with, even while she battled for her life. The hurricane of love hit everyone in its path.

Back home we had everything ready for Beth's arrival. Roy and I decided that we should test out the ramp. I put Roy in the wheelchair and ran him down the ramp. It worked almost too well. I started pushing a little too hard. I let go, and Roy had to use all of his racing skills to regain control of the wheelchair when he hit the driveway. We had a good laugh!

Around 2:30 p.m. on Tuesday, October 20, 2015, my Cakies returned home by ambulance. The medical personnel wheeled her up the ramp and put her in her own bed. She seemed happy to see all of the signs and balloons, and she was glad to be back in her home. I was so happy that I cried tears of joy. When I tried to give the ambulance workers a tip, they refused to take it. They said that it was their pleasure to bring Beth. Her attitude and kindness impressed them in the short time they were around her.

I had purchased a new grill in August, but I was waiting to use it. I wanted the first time to be when I grilled something for Beth, so Roy and I went to work on steak and chicken kabobs. Beth was excited to be home and wanted to come out to the living room to eat, so we got her out of bed and wheeled her out. She thoroughly enjoyed that meal. I loved seeing her eat so well. She hadn't had much of an appetite at all during her three weeks in the hospital.

I was thankful that I could finally sleep in the same bed with Beth again. We had a king size Sleep Number bed with an adjustable frame, so we kept her in our bed and used the hospital bed for other people to sit on while they were visiting her in the bedroom. Beth needed to sleep with her head, and her legs elevated because of the fluid that was in her body. The adjustable frame allowed us to get her into the proper position. I had a lot of trouble sleeping with the bed in that position, but I was determined to stay in bed with her. As long as Beth was comfortable, I was happy.

Beth was weak, and retaining fluid, which made her heavier—making it more difficult for her to stand and walk. She required help to get out of and into bed. During this time, I was never more grateful that Kirstyn had gone into nursing. She was able to provide expert care for her mother in many ways and was able to show me how to do the difficult tasks that needed to be done. Kirstyn's experience and expertise were invaluable during Beth's fight with cancer.

Dr. Gale had scheduled Beth's first platelet transfusion to take place at their Valley Forge facility for 1 p.m. that afternoon. The ambulance arrived to pick her up around 12:15 p.m. Roy needed to return home to Chicago, so he said his goodbyes and got on the road early that morning. Carol and I followed the ambulance in my car.

A nurse was already starting to give Beth the platelets when we arrived. She told me that her platelet count was close to 50,000 after her last infusion at the hospital. On this day, just two days later, her count was back down to only 17,000. The emotional roller coaster continued.

In the waiting room, I was approached by one of the physician's assistants who had seen Beth several times at this facility. She said, "What are you doing?"

I responded by saying, "Dr. Gale arranged for Beth to receive her platelets here."

She then said in a rather stern voice, "This will only prolong her life for a little while. You need to seriously consider hospice now." I realize that she probably thought Beth had been through enough, and was speaking from a heart of compassion. I just reminded this woman that Beth was under Dr. Gale's care and that we had an appointment scheduled for early November. I told her we were going to continue the platelet transfusions until then unless Beth changed her mind. I was completed exhausted emotionally, physically and spiritually, so I just left it at that and didn't say anything more.

If you are ever in the situation when a loved one won't give up a battle with illness that you think is lost, please consider your words carefully. Yes, patients and family deserve honesty, but at the same time, if the patient is not ready to give up yet, your words may cause more stress on a family that is already under a lot of pressure.

When Beth's platelet transfusion was complete, several of the nurses went into her room to hug her and wish her well. I recognized a nurse that had helped care for Beth before. I'm guessing that she was in her late-twenties. Her arms and neck were covered with tattoos and piercings. She liked Beth because Beth always took an interest in everything that was happening in her life. She made her feel loved and needed. This nurse was working with another patient, but she kept watching Beth as they wheeled her outside. I could tell that she wanted to say goodbye to Beth, but she wasn't sure if she should leave the patient she was helping at the moment. Finally, she told the patient that she'd be right back. She literally sprinted outside and gave Beth a huge hug just before they lifted her into the back of the ambulance. They spoke for a minute and then she ran back in. I saw tears in her eyes as she walked by. I think she had a strong sense that would be the last time that she would see Beth.

Beth had a profound effect on so many of the medical personnel who helped her along the way. Her love swept through offices, chemo suites, and hospitals. It was strong. It was real. It was a hurricane!

24

*B*eth's Final Decision

While driving back home that afternoon, I received a call from Caroline Stueck at QVC. She was checking in to see how things were going. I told her that we were in a very tough phase and that Beth was going to require full-time care now that she was home from the hospital. She suggested they pull me off the on-air schedule, and I agreed that it was time. I asked her to please tell all the hosts how grateful I was for their willingness to cover my shifts. She said they were happy to do it, and that I needed to focus on taking care of Beth.

By the time the ambulance arrived at our home, Beth was exhausted. She fell asleep early, and I wasn't far behind. In the middle of the night, Beth needed to use the commode. I was able to get her up in time, but as I was putting her back in bed her knees buckled, and she pulled me straight to the floor. I did my best to ease her down gently. Because her body had so much fluid, I couldn't lift her back up. Fortunately, I had told Beth's sister Carol to sleep with her phone by her ear in case I needed her. I called her, and she came down immediately. However, the two of us together weren't able to get Beth back up into bed. Someone had recently told me that in a situation like this I could call 911 and ask for a "lift assist." I called, and medical personnel arrived within fifteen minutes. They were able to lift Beth up and get her back into bed.

Thursday, October 22, 2015, was one of the hardest days of my life. Kirstyn came over that morning and bathed Beth, changed her nightie, and put lotion all over her. Around noon, Beth called us in and said that she didn't want to do any more treatments. It was evident to us that she was weary of the battle and ready to surrender. She said that she wanted hospice to come in and make her comfortable. She wanted to do the best she could to enjoy her final days.

You can't imagine what that felt like, unless you have experienced it. After battling cancer for three years, after countless doctor's visits, procedures, chemotherapy sessions, and pain medications, Beth decided to stop treatment. We all understood why she did it, but that didn't make it any easier to accept. One thing was certain; it wasn't our decision to make, it was hers. Beth was in charge.

We called hospice, and they came right away. We had a fantastic team of nurses to tend to Beth's needs and a very kind and caring social worker that sat down with us (in the living room out of Beth's hearing range) and explained what was going to happen. She told us their goal was to make Beth as comfortable as possible. The first thing they did was put in a catheter so that Beth wouldn't have to get out of bed. The second thing they did was to hook her up with a pack that would automatically deliver pain medication through her port whenever she needed it. The nurses came by at least twice a day to monitor her pain and medication. She said Beth would continue to fill with fluid and that eventually her organs would shut down and she would slip away. In her estimation, she would probably live for another week or two.

That meeting was heart-rending. But the phone call that followed was almost as tough. I had to call Dr. Gale to tell her that Beth was stopping her treatments. Her response was, "No

Dan! I can try to arrange to have the platelets delivered to your home if it's too hard for her to go to Valley Forge."

I stopped her and told her that this was completely Beth's decision. I explained that Beth had made it very clear this is what she wanted. Dr. Gale didn't say a word for a few seconds. She then told me, in a somber voice, that Beth was her favorite patient of her entire career as a doctor, and that our family had been a shining light to all who worked in her medical practice. She asked if she could speak with Beth before we hung up. I gave the phone to Cakies and told her it was Dr. Gale.

I could hear Dr. Gale's voice over the phone as she told Beth what an amazing woman she was, and that it had been her distinct honor to care for her. I had tears pouring down my face as Beth told her how blessed she was to have her as her doctor. She expressed her thanks for all that Dr. Gale and her entire team of physician's assistants and nurses had done for her and for all the love they had shown her. I will never forget the sadness I felt listening to that conversation. Even as I write this, the tears are once again running down my face.

After the hospice team left, I had some time alone with Beth. I asked her if she was anxious or scared, and she assured me that she wasn't. I told her that we should start bringing in her closest friends and family who wanted to see her one last time. I was struggling to grasp the fact that this was it. I then said to her, "Cakies you have always been the decorator in this family. God must have known you would need to go first and get our mansion ready. It won't be long, and I will be joining you, and we will then be together forever."

She told me she would do it. "I'll get our mansion ready Cakies," she said. She smiled and kissed me.

Our grandkids call Beth "Gam," and they call me "Papa." When we first became grandparents, we decided that grandma and grandpa sounded too old. Cole, our oldest grandson, was six years old at the time. He was very close to his Gam because he lived with us for the first year of his life. Beth took care of him whenever Kirstyn worked during his first three and a half years.

When Cole came home from school that day, Jeff and Kirstyn told him that Gam might be going to heaven soon to be with Jesus. They said to him that God must have needed an especially sweet angel and that is why Gam would have to go. Cole was so very sad. That little boy loved his Gam so much. He told his parents that he wanted to see her right away.

I was lying in bed next to Beth when Cole mustered up all of his courage and walked into the bedroom. He was crying, but he climbed up onto the bed and gave his Gam a big hug. He told her that she was the best Gam ever, and that he loved her very much. Beth always lit up around Cole and Gavin, and she gave him a big hug back and told him how much she loved him. My heart was breaking, and I couldn't keep from crying, so I left the room.

It was a warm fall night, so I went out onto our deck and sat down and just cried my eyes out. Kirstyn and Kelsey came out and sat beside me and held my hands. We hugged and cried and just held each other for a long time. After a while, Kirstyn said they were very concerned about me. She said that I should consider taking an anti-depressant to help me get through it. I didn't want to. I wanted to feel every emotion without being on a drug. Looking back, maybe I should have. I was an emotional wreck, but I felt like I needed to face the emotions head on.

I would not have made it through without the love and support of my family. I don't know how people make it through the loss of a spouse without the help of a loving family. We circled close and drew on each other's love for our strength.

Later that evening, we began calling Beth's family and her closest friends to tell them that Beth had stopped treatment. Beth's sister Carol decided to stay. Her daughters, Kim and Lisa, booked a flight to come and say goodbye to their favorite aunt. Her brother Roy decided to come back from Chicago with his wife, Paulette. We made arrangements to fly Beth's mom out right away.

Things had been so hectic for the last month that I rarely had time to ask anyone for help. However, with family and friends flying in from around the country I realized it was time to ask. I started calling friends to ask them to pick up people at the airport and bring them to our house. The Philadelphia airport is an hour away from my home, so this was a pretty big ask but every person I called said, "Yes. I'm glad to help." It seemed like I was randomly asking friends to pick people up but as it turned out I asked a school teacher to pick up a school teacher; musician to pick up a musician; nurse to pick up nurse, etc. It was quite amazing to look back and see how it all worked out.

25

Today was a Really Good Day

Our master bedroom became a prayer chapel during the last days of Beth's life. As family members and friends came to visit, we sang hymns of praise and worship in between times of prayer and conversation. Several of us knelt around Beth's bed from time to time to pray for her. I never stopped believing that God could heal her. I fully expected her to get out of that bed and start waiting on people the way she had always done before when we had company.

Beth's family arrived before the weekend, and they showered Beth with love. I told everyone to feel at home and find a place in the house to sleep. Somehow I think we used every bed, mattress, couch, and chair as a bed at some point. We had over fifteen people staying at our house.

Keeping Beth in our king size bed allowed everyone to crawl up next to her and hug her. We usually had Christian music playing, but once in a while, we switched to country because Beth was such a big fan of it.

The rash that had begun on her legs three weeks earlier now covered a good portion of her body and had even spread to her face. But somehow Beth managed to smile through it all. Her feet were itchy, so I spent a lot of time at the foot of the bed scratching them. She would lay her head back and smile as I did. I wasn't sleeping very much because of the way Beth had to have her head and feet elevated, so I regularly got out of bed in the middle of the night and knelt on the floor on her side of the bed and prayed.

One night I fell asleep while I was kneeling and I had a bizarre dream. I dreamed that I was in a hospital in a town in Southern Illinois, but I knew that I needed to get to Beth because she was having a procedure done in Philly. I was talking to her on the phone, and I told her I had no idea where I was, but somehow I would make it home in time to be with her before the procedure. I then found myself running through cornfields and flying over trees on my way there. I woke up while I was still running and flying. But I was happy that I was back with Beth because in the dream I had a horrible feeling of being separated from her at a critical time.

On Friday, October 23rd I woke up around eight o'clock in the morning. I was holding Beth's hand, and I didn't want to get out of bed. I knew once the day started, our room would fill up with people. I wanted to enjoy my time with her even though she was still asleep. I was looking straight ahead at our curtains covering the windows that face to the east. The sun was up, and I could see the shadow of the window slats on the curtain. They formed a perfect cross. As I was looking at one of the cross formations, I saw the shadow of a leaf above the cross fade into view. The point of the leaf was facing down toward the cross. This section of the curtain then began to glow, and the cross formation turned into a broader more rugged looking cross like the one that I imagine Christ was crucified on. It seemed like God was telling me to keep my mind and my eyes on Jesus.

Suddenly, I had a strong impression that I was supposed to get out of bed. I don't know why I did, but I got up and started walking toward the kitchen. As I walked by our front door, I heard a very faint knock. I would never have heard the knock from our bedroom. When I opened the door, I was surprised to see our neighbor, Darryl Goldsborough.

Darryl is a delightful guy. He and his wife, Alice, are wonderful Christian people who love the Lord with all their hearts. They have been a real source of encouragement to us over the years. They are very involved in their church and volunteer their time working with troubled youth.

When I opened the door, Darryl said, "Dan, I have hardly slept. I've been praying for Beth all night, and I feel like God is leading me to share something with her."

To many people this might seem strange, but I didn't question Darryl. I believed he did have an important and inspired message for Beth, because I knew that he was sincere and genuine in his faith. I told him to have a seat in the kitchen, and I would let Beth know. When I told Beth that Darryl wanted to talk to her, she was still in the process of waking up so she asked if she could clean up first. I asked Darryl if he could wait a while and he said he would wait as long as she needed. It took Carol and me about forty- five minutes to get Beth cleaned and changed. Darryl waited patiently in the kitchen the entire time.

When I brought him into the room, he exclaimed, "Beth I've got good news! This is a time for celebration because Jesus is present with you and you are going to be healed!" He then shared the story of the woman who had an issue with her blood from Matthew, chapter 9 in the Bible. This was profound in and of itself because Darryl didn't know that Beth's problem was with the platelets in her blood. Just like the lady in the story, she had an issue with her blood. In the Biblical account, the woman knows that Jesus is walking by, and she believes if she can touch His cloak, she will be healed. When Jesus sees her, and He knows that she touched Him, He tells her that her faith has healed her. Matthew wrote that she was healed from that moment on.

Darryl then looked her in the eyes and said, "Beth listen to me. If you get scared, close your eyes and picture Jesus, then reach out and touch Him. And remember, if God chooses to completely heal you now you will be able to get up out of this bed and enjoy the rest of your life with your family. But if God restores you to a perfect body in heaven, you will get to leave this mess of a world before the rest of us who are right behind you!"

Darryl's message was eloquent and filled with conviction. He spoke to Beth's heart. I had tears streaming down my face when he finished. Darryl is not a public speaker. He would tell you that he is not the most eloquent speaker. Darryl repairs and maintains helicopters, and he does his job exceptionally well, but speaking is not typically his strength. But on this day, he spoke so beautifully and so powerfully that it took us all by surprise. I believe that his message was divinely inspired that day. I walked him out of the house to the driveway. I had tears in my eyes as I hugged him and thanked him for being faithful to the Lord's leading and sharing such an important and personal message. He told me that he hadn't slept much the night before because he felt like he was supposed to give that message to Beth. When he woke up he was convinced that he needed to talk to her. He also told me that he was amazed at how well it turned out. He said, "That wasn't me speaking in there. You know that I can't talk like that!" I did indeed. I felt like I had witnessed another miracle.

Darryl's message spoke directly to Beth's heart. Her body was so full of fluid that it was very difficult for her to move at all. Her hands were swollen to twice their normal size. She couldn't lift her hands up to wipe a tear from her face. However, over the course of the next several days, there were many times when we saw her hands go straight up in the air. It appeared that she was reaching out to touch Jesus as He walked by. You could feel His presence in the room. We had witnessed the miracle of Darryl's eloquent message and the miracle of Beth lifting her swollen hands straight into the air when she was too weak physically to raise them. It was incredible!

I had been having a brutal time emotionally up until Darryl's visit. His message was mainly for Beth, but it spoke to me as well. As he spoke, I experienced an inexplicable peace come over me. In the storm of this horrible illness and the process of losing the one I loved the most, somehow I was surrounded by calm ... in the eye of the storm, at the center of it all.

The weather in southeast Pennsylvania was far from stormy that day. It was a "picture perfect" Friday in late October. People arrived at our house from out of town throughout the day. Beth's niece, Kim Bellone, flew in from California. Kim is an oncology nurse, and she was a tremendous blessing to her aunt and to all of us. She and Lisa always considered Beth to be their *cool aunt*. They always wanted to be like her. Watching Kim and Kirstyn take care of Beth during the next week was watching true love in action. They bathed her and rubbed lotion all over her skin every morning. They gave her the royal treatment that she so richly deserved. We were blessed to have two highly skilled nurses using their talents to love and care for Beth. The fact that they are cousins made it even more special.

Kirstyn, Kelsey and I started talking about Beth's memorial service. I have always disliked the term funeral, so I decided to call it *Beth's Celebration of Life Service*. We were trying to decide who would sing. We wanted the person to be someone who knew Beth well. Kelsey mentioned her childhood friend, Alyssa Boyd. I said, "Alyssa is the one. She would be perfect!"

Kelsey and Alyssa were best of friends in grade school, and Alyssa spent a lot of time at our house while she was growing up. She was always very outgoing and helped to pull Kelsey out of her shell. Even though she moved away in middle school, she and Kelsey had remained close friends. Alyssa always had a beautiful singing voice and with voice lessons she became an amazing singer. I asked Kelsey where Alyssa was living and she told me she was in Ohio. I asked her to please call her immediately. When Alyssa answered, I asked her if she would come and sing for Beth's service. She hesitated at first. I told her, "Alyssa, Beth was like a second mom to you, and this would be a way for you to honor her life."

She then said, "Yes. I will do it for Beth!"

I had been gathering lots of pictures and video, because I wanted to put together a visual presentation about Beth's life. But I knew that there was no way I would have the time to do it. I called another great friend, Oscar Dovale. Oscar was one of QVC's electronics experts. He knows more about electronics than anyone I have ever met. I asked him if there was any way he could put together a video about Beth's life that we could play at her service. He didn't hesitate. "Absolutely! I'd be glad to help!" he answered. You find out who your friends are in times like this. Oscar responded in the same way that my friend Bryan Law did when I asked him to build a ramp. He dropped everything and started working on Beth's video the next day.

Kirstyn, Jeff, Jeff's parents, Kelsey, Cole, Gavin, Beth's sister, Carol, and I were all in the bedroom with Beth that afternoon. We were trying to make the most of the precious little time we had left with her. We were all amazed at her calmness and her grace. She kept her spirits high even as she faced death.

One of Kirstyn's close friends from high school came over to see Beth that evening. Her name is Nicole Scotto. Nicole and Kirstyn started playing soccer together when they were six years old. They continued to play sports together through high school. We became close with Nicole's parents, Ray and Rose. When she came into our house, she gave me a big hug. She then hugged Kirstyn for a very long time. Nicole understood what Kirstyn was going through because her mom was also in a long, painful battle with cancer. (Her mom, Rose, passed away a year later.)

Nicole always thought of Beth as a second mom. When

she walked into the bedroom, she went directly to Beth's side, leaned over and gave her a hug that seemed like it lasted for several minutes. She told her what a beautiful woman she was and that she loved her so much. She was very emotional. She started to weep and, amazingly, Beth began to comfort her. It was sad, and yet it was beautiful. She told Beth everything that she came to tell her. She said that she was a fantastic mom and a terrific role model for her, Kirstyn and Kelsey. She didn't hold anything back.

If you are ever in a situation like this, say the things that you have always meant to say. It may be your last chance. Better yet, don't wait until a life and death situation to tell the people who matter the most to you that you love them.

Our friends Trish Whitnah and Dana Poirier picked up Beth's mom, Elaine, from the airport. They arrived at our house around 6 p.m. We were all anxious about Elaine. She and Beth were extremely close. They talked several times a day every day. I had flown her out to visit us a minimum of twice a year, for two weeks at a time, ever since we moved to Pennsylvania in 1991. Of course, she had called many times while Beth was in the hospital. When she arrived at the house that day, she immediately went to the bedroom to see her girl. She hugged her and loved on her for a very long time.

Before Trish and Dana left, they sat on the bed next to Beth and told her that they would help to take care of her family. At one point, Dana put Beth's face in her hands and said, "Listen. I love you, and I promise you that I will help take care of your girls and your grandkids."

I decided to let Beth's mom have some private time with her daughter after Trish and Dana left. I went out in the backyard to play with my grandsons, Cole and Gavin. They were a good distraction for me. While we were playing, a good buddy of mine named Joe Cafarcio came by. He is the saxophone player for Blue Sky band. Joe is a talented musician, but an even better human being. He brought a big box of soft pretzels for everyone to share. It was so good to see him. He told me that all the guys in the band sent their prayers and good wishes for my family. He lifted my spirits that day. Joe is another example of a good friend who just showed up.

Later that evening, we celebrated three birthdays. Gavin, Jeff and I all have birthdays in late October, so we decided to celebrate with cake and ice cream in the bedroom. Beth has always loved ice cream, and she made sure to have a taste of it that night. It was the saddest birthday any of us ever had, but at least we were all together. Kirstyn and Kelsey got a card for Beth to sign to me. She could barely write her name because her hands were so swollen.

Beth was exhausted from all the visitors that day, so it didn't take her long to fall asleep after everyone left the room. I knelt down by her side of the bed, laid my hands on her and prayed for a long time. It was another terrible night for me emotionally. I remember looking at her while she slept. The cancer and the chemo had taken their toll on her. The rash had spread to cover her entire body and some of her face. She was extremely swollen from the fluid. I remember asking God, "Why? Why did this have to happen to Beth?" She was the sweetest, kindest, most loving person I knew. I didn't understand, but I believed that God could still heal her and raise her up out of that bed if He chose to do so. I didn't fall asleep until the wee hours of the morning. It is hard to sleep when you know your wife is dying, and the time is short.

At some point in the early hours of the morning, I must have crawled into bed. I remember looking at the clock through blurry eyes and not fully comprehending where I was and what day it was. The beautiful thing about sleep is that it makes us forget about our troubles for a while. There were many mornings during this time that I woke up hoping that Beth's cancer was a bad dream, but reality quickly shattered that hope.

I finally figured out that the clock was telling me it was 9 a.m. on Saturday, October 24th, 2015. I decided to stay in bed as long as I could. This was becoming a habit because I knew that once everybody was awake, I had to share Beth. I treasured the time I had with her alone. I just looked at her and prayed for her until she woke up. Kirstyn and Kim liked treating her to a long, luxurious bath first thing in the morning, so that was my cue to get out of bed.

When I walked into the kitchen to get my morning coffee, I saw Jeff, my son- in-law. I thought that I needed a distraction so I asked him if he would help me put the deck and patio furniture into the shed. He said he'd be glad to. This was never an easy task, so "glad to" probably wasn't accurate, but we waded into the project. My shed is not big enough to hold all of the stuff that I try to put into it. Every fall I have to take everything out and rearrange the entire shed so I can put all the chairs, umbrellas and tables back in. I had hoped this would be a good distraction from all of the heaviness, but I was wrong. As we were putting away all of the furniture, I realized that when I took it all back out in the spring, Beth was not going to be here.

Kelsey came out at one point and asked me to listen to a song that she thought would be perfect for the video of Beth's life: "I Will See You Again" by Carrie Underwood. I listened to about two measures and just started crying like a baby. It is a beautiful song, and I knew it would be perfect. It was so sad to think that Beth wasn't going to be with us much longer, but I was confident that I would see her again.

A huge, beautiful bouquet of flowers arrived that afternoon with a card that said, "To Beth with much love, the girls from Kelly's." Kelly's was Beth's favorite breakfast and lunch spot. We had been regulars there for about four years. Everyone who worked there loved her and knew about her battle. She perked up when she saw the flowers.

Beth had many friends from all walks of life. She could

always win anyone over even if they were mean-spirited. We had a neighbor who was in his eighties. He had a reputation for being cantankerous, and we soon discovered this reputation was well earned. He complained about everything. When we first moved in, he complained that our house blocked his view of the sunset. I often reminded him that I didn't build the house I just bought it! He visited us on a regular basis to complain that our kids were too noisy. After I mowed the lawn, he usually complained that I accidentally came over a few inches onto his lawn. He told me in no uncertain terms that I needed to learn where the boundary marker was. He just liked to complain. Slowly but surely Beth won this man over. I'll never forget coming home from work one night and hearing a man's voice in our family room. I walked in and there he was, having coffee and cookies with Beth. My jaw about hit the floor. He kept telling us story after story and we thought he'd never leave!

As this man grew older, his son, Gary, came over to help him take care of his lawn. Gary and Beth soon became great friends. They loved to sit and talk out on our deck during the warm summer months.

Gary peaked into the shed as Jeff and I were organizing it on this late October afternoon. He asked me how Beth was doing. I told him that she was not doing well. He was heartbroken when I informed him that Beth had decided to stop all treatment. His eyes filled with tears as he told me that my wife was "the most wonderful person he had ever known." About an hour later another bouquet of flowers showed up at our door from him. I walked over to his yard and told him that Beth appreciated the flowers and that she wanted me to tell him that she loved him. He asked if there was any way he could peak his head into the room to tell her how much he thought of her. I brought him into the house and asked Beth if he could say hello. She said it would be okay. I don't remember his exact words, but I know that he thanked her for being such a good friend to him and for showing him so much love.

Friends and family kept arriving throughout the weekend. The gathering of people in our room kept growing. There was a beautiful sense of peace and calm in the room. Hymns were usually playing in the background as people said their goodbyes to Beth.

Sherry Dickey came by with another friend from our kids' soccer days, Betty Veneziale. They sat and shared great memories of soccer trips, proms and other fun times. Beth smiled and laughed as they reminisced. I kept wondering what she was thinking. She knew she was dying yet she seemed to be at peace. I am convinced that God gave her that peace because she knew she was going to be in heaven for eternity. She had done her best to spread God's love to everyone she met. She had found complete peace in the eye of her hurricane of love.

Shortly after Betty and Sherry left, George Veneziale, Betty's husband, arrived from the airport with Beth's other niece from California, Lisa Bellone. This was an example of how I inadvertently put people of similar occupations together. George and Lisa were both teachers, so they had a lot to talk about on their ride from the airport.

I was relieved that Beth's family had all arrived now to see her. Her mom, her sister, and her two nieces were in our home and her brother, Roy, had been with her the week before. He was now on his way back out with his wife, Paulette. I was glad that everyone in her family had made it out to say goodbye. There were times during these final days when I thought what if Beth dies and I waited too long to bring people in? I would have lived with that regret the rest of my life.

With so many people in the house, it was impossible to wait on people. The refrigerator and freezer were stuffed full of food, so we told people to help themselves to any of the food when they were hungry.

Around dinner, I was happy to discover that it was just Beth and me in the room. I lied down next to her and just held her for about a half-hour when Kelsey came in. She crawled up next to Beth and gave her a big hug. Suddenly, Kelsey started crying uncontrollably. She said, "Mommy this isn't fair. I'm sorry I'm not strong right now. I love you so much. Who am I going to tell everything to when you're gone? I tell you everything!" Beth just hugged her for a long time. Kirstyn came in and hugged both of them.

She looked at Kelsey and said, "Kelsey, we are so fortunate. I tell people all the time that we have the best parents in the world. We are so lucky that we were born into this family. I have no regrets because we tell each other that we love each other all the time."

This was an extraordinary moment in time for our family. Beth, Kirstyn, Kelsey and I were all together. It was just the original four. For the next hour, we shared family stories some of which I heard for the first time as we reminisced. I discovered how Beth protected the girls by not telling me about certain things they did that would have caused me to "hit the roof." One example was a time when Kelsey was too sick to go to school for a couple of days. At the time, Beth told me she thought Kelsey had the flu. What had, in fact, happened: Kelsey was at a party and drank too much. I never knew she had even tasted alcohol. We had our own little "true confession time."

After the confessions, Kirstyn asked Beth if she would record a message for us that we would be able to play whenever we missed her. I got out my phone and started recording. In her weak voice, Beth said, "I love you so much. I love you guys so much. You're in my heart, and I'm in your heart forever, forever and ever. I love you." I'm so glad that we made that recording. I play it often when I want to feel close to her. It brings back all the emotion of that moment, however, as the three of us can be heard crying in the background.

Recently, I listened to this recording, and I realized that Beth was consoling us. She was the one who was dying and yet she kept assuring us that everything would be okay. At one point, she looked at Kelsey and told her that it was okay to cry because she needed to let her emotions come out. Kelsey asked, "But who will give me hugs when you are gone? Mommy, you give the most comforting hugs. Nobody gives hugs like you!" Beth then told her she could always hug a pillow.

Kirstyn asked, "Did you say hug a pillow? That won't come close to replacing your hugs!" Kirstyn then told Kelsey that she could come over to her house whenever she needed a hug.

It wasn't long before the room once again filled with people. But I'm thankful for that short time when it was only the four of us talking openly and honestly and expressing our feelings for each other. That will always be a special memory for Kirstyn, Kelsey and me.

When everybody came back into the room, the mood lightened. In fact, it started to feel like a celebration. People were exhausted, so maybe they just started acting silly. Or perhaps the heaviness was too much. I remember looking at Beth wondering what she was thinking. She genuinely seemed to be enjoying the moment with everyone in the room. We all shared funny stories about her and for a few moments, it seemed like we were having a fun family reunion. Finally, one by one, people began to leave the room to find their bed.

When everyone left, I crawled into bed. It was late, so I leaned over and gave Beth a kiss. As I laid my head down, she said, "Cakies, today was a good day. Today was a really good day." I told her that it was indeed. I smiled because I realized that even though she was dying of cancer, she was still able to say that it was a really good day. What an incredible attitude! What a profound lesson for all of us!

When you crawl into bed each night think about the good things that happened to you that day. Like Beth, focus on the positive even on your worst day. If you think about your blessings, you too will be able to say, "Today was a good day. Today was a really good day!"

26

An Angel in our Driveway

When Beth decided to stop her treatments, one of the first people I called was my close friend, Brian Roland, who lived in California. He told me that he was ready to come whenever I needed him to. I called him on Friday night—he was at my house the next night. Brian loves music and is a musician and singer. Without thinking about it, I sent the lead singer from Blue Sky Band, my great friend, John Spangenberg, to pick up Brian at the airport. When they arrived at the house, I went outside and met them in the driveway. The three of us were talking, along with John's sweet wife, Joey. I noticed that John wasn't very talkative, but I just figured he was tired.

After John and Joey left, I asked Brian if John had talked much on the way from the airport. Brian said they talked nonstop the entire way. I said that John must have been tired by the time they got to the house because he didn't say much when we were all chatting in the driveway. I didn't give it another thought.

The next day Brian came into the bedroom to say hello to Beth. She was happy to see him. Brian and I were roommates in Chicago when Beth and I first met. The three of us spent a lot of time together in those early days. Brian loved Beth like she was family.

One of the first things Brian wanted to do was pray for her. We both knelt by her bed, and he prayed a beautiful, sincere prayer, asking God to comfort her and touch her in a unique way. After he finished praying, we started singing choruses and hymns.

My sister, Janie, and my brother-in-law, Ronn Read, arrived that afternoon, after driving twelve hours straight from Wauconda, Illinois. They had just returned from Africa the night before they left—barely had time to unpack and repack in between trips. Ronn is our family pastor. He performs our marriages and funerals and does lots of counseling with all of us in between. When they walked into the bedroom to see Beth for the first time, Ronn sat down on the bed next to her and asked, "How are you doing?"

She paused for a few moments and then said, "I'm sad, but I'm not afraid." She said that she didn't want to leave us but that she knew where she was going, and she knew she would be ok.

Over the next several days, Beth often stared up at the right corner of the ceiling. Her eyes seemed fixated on a specific spot. One day I asked her what she was seeing. Even though her voice was weak, she very clearly said, "Heaven!"

I asked, "Is it beautiful, Cakies?"

She nodded and said, "Yes!"

When I awoke on Monday, I quickly realized two things. First, it was my sixty-first birthday and secondly, God had granted me my birthday wish. During Beth's third week in the hospital, I began asking God for a birthday present. I wanted to have Beth back home for my birthday. He gave me that present. I just wanted to hang onto that moment before the day began.

When I walked out to the kitchen to get a cup of coffee, my sister, Janie, was sitting at the counter. She said, "You need to call John Spangenberg! He saw something!" I had no idea what she was talking about, so she explained that Dana, our neighbor, had talked to John, and he told her that he needed to speak to me. He apparently saw *something* that he needed to tell me about, the night he picked Brian up at the airport. I called John, and he said he needed to talk to me for a few minutes as soon as possible. I told him to come by later after he finished working.

I kept wondering what John had seen, so I was looking forward to speaking to him. For some reason, I met him in the Poirier's driveway. He had his vintage Datsun convertible with the top down. I hopped into the passenger side of his car and said, "What's up? What did you see?"

He started speaking very deliberately and said, "Now, I don't want you to think I'm crazy, because this is going to sound strange. But I know what I saw."

I said, "O.K., I'm ready! What did you see?"

He proceeded to say, "As you were talking the other night, this being appeared right behind you."

I interrupted and said, "What do you mean by a being?"

"He was probably about eight to nine feet tall, and he was standing right over you. It looked like he was wearing a robe with a hood, but I couldn't see his face because he was so bright. In fact, I couldn't look at him for very long without looking away because the light hurt my eyes. It was a dazzling light that seemed to dance or sparkle. I looked away, and when I looked back, he was gone. But as you talked, he appeared again. I could only look for a few seconds then I had to close my eyes. This time when I looked back, he was gone, and he didn't appear again," he responded.

I didn't say anything for a few seconds as I was taking this all in. Finally, I looked at him and asked, "What or whom do you think it was?"

He confidently said, "I think it was an angel."

I paused and then responded, "So do I, John. With all of the prayer and praise that has been going on in my house, I have no doubt that there are angels all around it."

After John left, I walked home and stood in the exact spot

where I was standing when John saw this being. I turned around and tried to imagine what he saw. I was a little envious thinking that he actually might have seen an angel. He was given a gift, and so was I. After all, it was my sixty-first birthday.

27

Final Goodbyes

When I came back into the house, my family surprised me with a birthday cake. They put just a few candles on it because sixty-one might have started a wildfire! We are always told to make a wish before we blow out the candles. My only wish was that God would completely heal Beth so we could keep her around.

As I looked around the room, I realized that Beth had brought everyone together as she had always done. The most significant difference this time was that she wasn't the one waiting on people as she had always done in the past. She always made sure everyone else was happy. Now it was our turn to wait on her. But she still couldn't stop worrying about everybody else. At one point, she asked Kirstyn, "What if all these people came to see me and I don't die?"

Kirstyn started laughing and said, "Oh mom we won't be disappointed! Trust me. We'll throw a big party and celebrate the fact that you are staying with us!"

By 11 p.m. everyone started heading off to bed. For the first time in several weeks, I fell asleep right away. The problem was I woke up at midnight and then watched the clock until six in the morning. I may have slept for another hour and a half after that.

When I woke up, I touched Beth's face and gently kissed

her on the cheek. I started crying as I thought about how sad it was that after thirty- seven years we might only have a few days left together on this earth. She suddenly opened her eyes and asked me why I was crying. I didn't want to make her sad, so I said that I was crying because I was happy she was home to help me celebrate my birthday. I then whispered, "Cakies, you're my hero."

She looked at me a moment and then said, "You're mine!" We hugged and held each other for a long time.

Beth touched people's hearts wherever she went. She was intensely loyal, so once you were her friend, you were her friend for life. She went to the same hair stylist for fifteen years—and became close friends with her. The woman's name is Becky. Kirstyn also became a client of Becky's somewhere along the way and she asked her if she could come by the house to cut her hair.

Naturally, Becky wanted to say goodbye to Beth, too, and came to the house to cut Kirstyn's hair and see Beth one final time. After she cut Kirstyn's hair, she offered to cut mine as well. When you are caring for a loved one, taking care of your appearance falls low on your priority list, so I was happy for the offer. As she was working on my hair, she told me how much she loved and adored Beth. She echoed the words of so many others, saying that Beth was the kindest, most loving, loyal, and joyful person she had ever met. Becky's sweet words reminded me how fortunate I was to be married to Beth for thirty-one years.

Before Becky left, she went into the bedroom and had a long talk with Beth, kissing her and giving her a big hug. I walked her out to the living room and saw tears streaming down her face. I hugged her and thanked her for coming. She said, "I would do anything for any member of your family because of Beth. She is such a special person. I will miss her so much!"

To have great friends, you must be a great friend. Beth was the best friend anyone could have. The impact of her love was immeasurable. Unfortunately, the greater the love is the greater the pain and sadness when it is time to say goodbye. It was excruciating to watch friends and family say their final goodbyes to Beth. But the hardest were still to come.

There was a lot of prayer and praise going on in our home that day. I was sitting next to Beth singing along to a Christian song that was playing when Beth suddenly exclaimed, "Cakies, I want to see Miss Deb!" She was referring to our dear friend, Deb Cortese. Deb and her husband, Vic, were among the first friends we made when we moved to Pennsylvania. We used to get together with them and a couple in our neighborhood named Barb and Duane Rehmeyer. Our kids were all about the same ages, so we enjoyed pool time and barbecues.

I called Deb and told her that Beth was asking for her. She said she would drop everything and come right over. Deb was another one who considered Beth her best friend. I told her that Beth hadn't asked to see anyone specifically but her. She stayed all afternoon and evening, and when she hugged Beth goodbye my heart broke a little bit more.

After Deb left, I walked out onto the deck to get some fresh air. My emotions were out of control, and I didn't want to add to Beth's sadness. As I looked up at the moon, I was struck by how full and bright it was. It was Tuesday, October 27, 2015, and it was a full moon for the ages. As I stared at it, I prayed again and asked God to give us all strength for the next day when Beth's nieces, Kim and Lisa, were scheduled to fly back to California. I knew those would be the hardest goodbyes yet.

It seemed to me like Beth was hanging on to life to make sure she said all of her goodbyes. I also think she didn't want to leave on any of our birthdays. Gavin's and mine had passed, and Jeff's was coming up on the 31st. She was growing weaker by the day, and it was getting harder for her to speak.

Even in her weakened condition, she was always concerned

about me. She looked at me one day and said, "Oh Cakies, this is so hard on you isn't it?"

I said, "Only because I love you so much and I want you around. You are my love, my best friend, and my rock."

Then I remembered something my brother-in-law Ronn had told me. He said that I needed to tell her it was ok for her to go. So I looked at her and said, "Cakies, I want you to know that it is ok for you to go when you're ready. You have taught me well, and I promise you I will take care of everything and everyone."

I took a short break from the bedroom later that day and walked out to the kitchen to get a glass of water. All of a sudden, Kelsey came running out of the bedroom and yelled, "Dad! Mom wants you right away!"

I went sprinting down the hallway and knelt down by her side of the bed and said, "What is it Cakies?"

She looked at me and said, "Eat! I want you to eat something!" I kissed her and told her I would eat a sandwich right away! She was always thinking of others even as she was dying.

Beth's sense of humor stayed intact to the very end. During one particularly poignant moment, I was telling Beth not to worry about a thing when she was gone, because I had it all under control. In the middle of all of my promises, she interrupted me and said, "Cakies, you have bad breath." Kelsey was sitting on the bed, and Beth looked at her and started laughing. She thought that was so funny. I hadn't seen her laugh this hard for several months. Since I had her laughing, I decided to humor her more so I ran into the bathroom, brushed my teeth, rinsed with mouthwash and gargled really loudly. I came back and kissed her, and she said, "Oooohhhh, much better!" She looked at Kelsey and said, "Poor Daddy!" and then laughed some more.

We needed those moments of comic relief because the rest of the day was emotionally draining. Her nieces, Kim and Lisa, had to leave, so they came in to say goodbye. They took turns crawling up on the bed next Beth to hug and kiss her. They told her how much they loved her and how much she meant to them. Kim and Lisa said that growing up, Beth was always their "cool aunt." They told her that they both wanted to be like her then, but now, as adults, they wanted to be like her even more. My heart hurt so badly that day, and as I write this, I feel that deep sadness once again.

When I walked them out of the bedroom, Kim and Lisa both broke down and sobbed. Each one had taken some of their Auntie Beth's clothes, they said, so they could wrap themselves up in her love when they missed her. There were tears as they left us—and tears falling all the way to the airport and during their long flight home.

That was one of the most terrible days of my life. I think it was for our entire family. I don't know how Beth did it. She knew that she was saying her final goodbyes to the people she loved the most in this world.

Can you imagine how this would feel? Is there someone who comes to mind that you need to get things right with? Is there someone that you need to call today and tell them that you love them? Don't wait for that final goodbye. Remember, nobody gets out of here alive. The percentage for death is one hundred percent. One hundred people out of every one hundred people born are going to die. Don't wait until they are gone. Tell them you love them today!

28

*B*eth's Final Journey

Cancer is not pretty. It is ugly and cruel. But Beth's beauty never faded, in spite of what was happening to her body. Her spirit was beyond beautiful, and so was her smile. I don't think that I will ever understand why she went through what she did. However, I still trust the Lord, and I know that He loves me and that He loves Beth very much. I believe that I will understand when I get to heaven and see Him face to face.

After Beth's nieces left, her breathing became noticeably more difficult. She slowed to five to six breaths per minute. Her "rattle" became more pronounced. I had always heard about the death rattle, but I had never actually heard it until now. Kirstyn gave her a pill to help with the heavy congestion in her lungs that was caused by the build-up of fluid. She also gave her a flavored sponge to help with the dryness in her mouth.

All of the family and friends in the house were together in the bedroom singing praise and worship songs throughout the day. At one point, everybody stopped singing because little Cole came in the room. He crawled up by his Gam. Beth was fairly unresponsive all day, but when she opened her eyes and saw Cole, she rallied. She kissed him and told him she loved him. I have always heard that love is the most powerful force on earth.

All of us in the room that day witnessed it. Everyone who ever came in contact with Beth felt that powerful force.

Every night when I crawled into bed, I wondered if it would be my last night on earth with Beth by my side. When I kissed her on this night, I started crying. She told me to stop and to go to sleep because she wasn't leaving yet. Her strength, her determination, her spirit, and her will were incredible. She assured me that I could fall asleep knowing that she would still be with me the next day.

On the morning of Wednesday, October 28, 2015, I wrote the following in my journal, "I have a strong sense that today may be the day that Beth leaves us." She didn't. She wasn't ready. It wasn't her day to go.

The weather may have influenced my thinking. It was Indian summer in southeast Pennsylvania. Most of the days that October were warm and sunny. But this day was rainy and gloomy.

Cole brought his six- year- old sunshine into the room later in the day with a beautiful card he made for his Gam. Beth lifted up her swollen hand and touched it. She told Cole that it was beautiful then she told him that she loved him, and hugged and kissed him. Cole and Gavin also brought her little pumpkins they painted for her. She loved these little guys so much and really lit up around both of them.

The love continued to pour in from friends and family. Trish Whitnah brought over another generous helping of delicious home cooked food. After she loaded up the refrigerator, she stopped in to see Beth and told her not to worry about a thing because she was going to help take care of her girls. Four of my band mates from Blue Sky called to encourage me. Dave Long, Todd Pohlig, Dave Glarner and John Bergh, all called to say that they were praying for us.

Beth asked to see a few more friends. Barb Rehmeyer and her daughters, Sam and Stephanie, came by. They had become a part of our extended family over the years. They all loved Beth. Friends kept stopping by throughout the day, but most of our family stayed with Beth all day. We knew she was getting ready to leave.

My brother-in-law, Ronn, came into the bedroom around one o'clock in the afternoon. He was talking on his phone, and he signaled for me to follow him out of the room. I was upset because I thought he wanted me to talk to someone. I had spent too much time on the phone already and didn't want to talk to anyone else. I just wanted to stay with Beth. I reluctantly followed him out to the kitchen. He pointed to the tree outside the kitchen window. There was a beautiful, bright red cardinal sitting in the tree by our empty bird feeder. The amazing thing was that it was pouring rain outside. I had never seen a red cardinal sit in a tree during a downpour. Yet there he was! He sat in that tree throughout the afternoon. He didn't move from that spot for several hours! I thought that God had sent that cardinal because he was either going to heal Beth or take her to heaven that afternoon.

It must not have been God's time or Beth's because, once again, she rallied! She sat up in bed and asked for Mexican food! So Brian made burritos for dinner. We brought her one and she took a couple of bites and then burped out loud and laughed. To our amazement she ate the entire burrito! Once again, she told Kirstyn that she was worried that she might not die after all of these people had come to see her. Once again Kirstyn assured her that no one would be disappointed if she didn't die. My Cakies always worried about everyone else.

Throughout the late afternoon and evening, Beth kept staring up at the right side of the ceiling. Periodically, she would wave and smile in that direction. I asked her again what she was seeing. She said, "I see heaven."

"Is it beautiful?" I asked.

"Yes!" she answered.

At one point, I noticed that her eyes filled with tears. I wiped them from her face and asked her if she was okay. She nodded yes. All of a sudden, she tried to get out of bed. She swung her legs out to her left side and said that she had to go to the bathroom. I just reacted without thinking and started running downstairs to get the commode.

Kirstyn brought me back to my senses by calling, "Dad! She is not getting out of bed! She has a catheter in, and she hasn't been out of bed for several days!"

Beth then started saying, "I need to go outside to see Dawnie! She's out there on the deck!" She was referring to my sister, Dawn, who was not on the deck but at her home in Quincy, Illinois.

We finally got her settled down, and Kirstyn and I got her ready to go to sleep. We changed her bed pad and put a clean pajama nightie on her. Sometimes people get a final surge of energy in their last days. I think that is what happened, because Beth was quiet for the remainder of the evening. We noticed that she kept looking up at that spot in the corner of the ceiling. Her eyes seemed fixed on one area. We wondered what she was seeing, and wished that we could see it too. Once again, as she closed her eyes, she lifted her hand straight up in the air as if she was trying to touch the hem of Jesus' garment. This was amazing because she was barely able to lift her hands off the bed during the day.

After Beth fell asleep, Kirstyn started going through some of the packages that were accumulating in our sitting room. We were so preoccupied caring for Beth that whenever a package came, we just threw it on the floor with the other boxes. The place was starting to fill up. Suddenly, Kirstyn came into the living room sobbing. She was holding a Gluten- Free Cookbook that she found in one of the packages. Beth had ordered it from QVC to give to Kirstyn for Christmas because Cole needed to eat a gluten-free diet to help with inflammation. In spite of the advanced stage of her cancer, Beth was still buying Christmas gifts. It was a reminder of her love for her family even as she was dying. It touched Kirstyn in such a way that she let out some deep emotions. Ronn and I hugged her and tried to comfort her. Ronn told her she needed to have faith to believe that everything was going to be all right. He told her to look at the tattoo on her left wrist that reads "Faith." Beth had a tattoo in the same spot that said, "Love" and Kelsey has one that says, "Hope." Together they form faith, hope, and love.

Beth's breathing became more labored throughout the night. She seemed to moan with each breath. I finally fell asleep around midnight but woke up early the next morning. When I looked over at Beth, I was surprised that she was awake. Her eyes were open and fixed on the same spot in the upper right corner of the ceiling. Suddenly, I heard her say, "Hi" in a pleasant voice, as she continued to look up. A few seconds later she said, "Hello!"

I asked, "Who do you see Cakies?" She shrugged her shoulders and smiled. It seemed like she knew that I couldn't see whomever it was that she was greeting.

Kirstyn was in the room with us at the time. A little bit later and we heard Beth say, "Hi daddy!" Kirstyn asked her if she saw her dad. Again, Beth just smiled. Her dad, Bud Johnson, passed away in 1968...his pastor told us Bud had asked Jesus to come into his heart before he died. I believe he may have been greeting his daughter from heaven.

I wanted to make sure I told Beth everything I was feeling in my heart because I knew the end was near. She was having trouble communicating at this point, but she was still aware of everything. I told her that she made my life complete, and I thanked her for loving me like nobody else ever did. I noticed tears welled up in her eyes, so I gently wiped them away and told her that I loved her with all of my heart.

Beth's sister, Carol, had to leave in the afternoon to fly back to California. She came into our room while it was still early morning. I let them have some time alone. I came back about twenty minutes later with a cup of coffee. The morning was always a special time for Beth and me. I usually woke up first and then brought her coffee and a muffin while she was still in bed. We would sit in bed and drink our coffee together and ease into the day. I realized that she was looking at my coffee mug and I said, "Cakies, do you want some coffee?" She nodded, so I ran into the kitchen and got her a straw. She had a few sips and smiled. It made me smile. It was the last time we had coffee together.

Beth and I told each other we loved each other all the time. We would squeeze each other's hands three times to say it when we couldn't speak. By this point, Beth was unable to speak or squeeze my hand, so when I would tell her that I loved her, she blinked her eyes three times to tell me she loved me too.

Carol spent the rest of the morning rubbing Beth's head and looking at old photos of the two of them. Beth couldn't talk, but she was listening as Carol told funny stories and showed her the photos. When she hugged and kissed her goodbye, we were all sobbing. She took some of Beth's clothes to wrap up in when she missed her, and left for the airport, crying all the way. She later told me that she was so sad that day, but so grateful to have had the time with Beth. She said she just felt numb on the long flight back to California.

We all spent the rest of that day in the bedroom together. Kirstyn, Kelsey, Elaine, Roy, Paulette, me, Brian, Ronn, Janie, Jeff, Gavin, Cole, Ed and Nancy Hauser were all there. We talked, prayed and sang worship songs. Beth slept most of the day. Her breathing was very labored, and her rattle was sounding worse. I wrote in my journal that we sang Beth's favorite hymn, "Victory in Jesus". That evening, we sang "I Surrender All". On a couple of occasions, I briefly escaped to our master bathroom to ask God to take her peacefully and not to let her suffer anymore.

My nieces, Terra and Noelle, Ronn and Janie's daughters, arrived in town that night. They stopped by our house for a while before going to the Poirier's home to sleep. Our neighbors, Dana and Steve, opened up their home to our family and friends from out of town—Someone was already sleeping on every bed, couch, chair, and floor space in our home. I remember thinking that it was a shame that we waited so long to have a big family reunion at our home, and that it was under such trying circumstances. Beth always brought us together, and she had brought us together once again.

This was a terrible day for all of us, but it was especially hard for Kelsey. I think the weight of losing her mother started hitting her full force. I remember she cried hard throughout the day and my heart broke for her. It broke for all of us.

For some reason, I asked Kirstyn if she would sleep on the hospital bed in our bedroom that night. I was worried that if Beth passed in the night, I wouldn't know what to do. She said she would. We went to sleep around 10:30 p.m.

At around 3 a.m. Beth let out a loud, long moan. It was so loud that Kelsey came running down from her bedroom upstairs. For some strange reason, nobody else in the house heard it. It was so loud that it seemed to come from deep inside of Beth's body. She was completely unconscious at the time. The three of us watched her for a while. We heard the rattle with every breath she took. I felt like she might leave before morning. I didn't sleep much that night.

When the light of day woke me in the morning, I immediately checked on Beth to make sure she was still breathing. She was. When I looked at the clock, it was 8:04 a.m. I had a pretty good idea that this would be the day of her homecoming.

Terra and Noelle came over first thing in the morning. The last time they had seen their aunt Beth was in May of 2011 at their cousin Zach's wedding. Zach is the son of my youngest sister, Dawn and her husband, Glenn. That was a year and five months before we learned that Beth had cancer. We had danced at the reception well into the night. Beth felt and looked great at that time. Terra and Noelle were shocked to see how she looked on this day, but they were glad they came. They decided that they would come at the last minute, and they got the last two seats on the plane.

Beth appeared to be in a deep state of unconsciousness by this point, and her breathing had slowed even further. She was now taking only three to four breaths a minute. Kirstyn, Kelsey, Elaine, and I stayed by her all day. Kelsey was lying next to Beth on her left side and Kirstyn was on her right. They were hugging Beth, and I was embracing all three of them from her right. Beth's mom, Elaine, was sitting in a chair next to the bed, caressing Beth's face. We spoke positive affirmations to her throughout the day. We kept telling her how much we loved her and how we were so blessed to have her in our lives. I remember saying that she was the Blue Ribbon, First Prize, the Gold Standard of wives and moms, and that we were so fortunate to have her in our lives. We also told her that she could go whenever she was ready. I kept promising her that I would take care of our family and carry on the way that she taught me—with lots of love.

Shortly after 2 p.m., Kirstyn texted Susan Oddo, our neighbor, to ask if she could come by to change Beth's pain cartridge. Susan was a hospice nurse at the time. She adored Beth and was always checking on her to see if she needed anything. In fact, when we decided to call in hospice, we wanted Susan to be Beth's nurse, but her organization didn't think that was a good idea because of their close relationship. Susan, however, told us to text her if we needed anything. I remember talking to her at the end of our driveway about a month earlier, when Beth's health was deteriorating rapidly. It was just before her final three-week stay in the hospital. Susan had cried as she spoke about my wife. She'd told me that Beth was one of the sweetest, kindest people she had ever met in her life. She said, "Beth instantly made me feel like I belonged, as soon as we moved into the neighborhood. She welcomed me with open arms and an open heart."

Susan walked into our bedroom about fifteen minutes after Kirstyn called. She could tell that Beth was getting ready to go. Her breathing was very labored, but now her breaths became very short and very fast. We held her tighter and continued to tell her how much we loved her. Kelsey said, "I will see you soon Mommy." Susan pulled out the empty pain medicine cartridge, and, as if on cue, Beth breathed her last. She coughed, and just like that, she was gone. It happened in an instant.

I looked at the clock, and it was 2:40 p.m., October 30th, 2015. It happened in the blink of an eye. We stayed there just holding her for a while. I kissed her on the cheek. Her face was still warm. Kirstyn, Kelsey, and Elaine kissed her. We all told her that we loved her forever. Then we all got up and left the room. Our lives would never be the same. I had never been with someone when they passed from this earth into heaven. It was an incredible honor to be with Beth when she did.

I walked out onto our deck while Ronn, Janie, Terra, and Noelle went into the bedroom to help Susan tend to Beth. I remember being amazed at how beautiful the weather was. It was sunny with temperatures in the seventies. It was as if nature was celebrating Beth's life while we were overwhelmed with grief. Kirstyn and Kelsey went upstairs for a while and then joined Elaine, and me outside on the deck as they took Beth out of the house. We held each other and wept for a long time. There seemed to be no end to our tears.

We'd had three years to consider the possibility that this day would come. During the entire month of October, it looked like a certainty that it would come. Still, there is no way to prepare for it when it happens. I felt like someone had just delivered a knockout punch to my jaw and ripped out my heart. Part of me was relieved that my Cakies was finally out of her pain. But the heartache that came with the realization that I would never see my wife on earth again was almost unbearable. The agony of looking at Kirstyn and Kelsey and realizing their mom wouldn't be here for all of life's special moments seemed overwhelming. I thought about Cole and Gavin not having their Gam to watch them grow up. My mind was in a million places, but my heart was with Beth. Part of me wanted to go with her that day. I think part of me did.

I don't know how long we were on the deck. I guess for most of the afternoon. At one point, I realized that I needed to call someone in the talent department at QVC. I reached Caroline Stueck by phone and shared the news that Beth was gone. I could hear the hurt and disappointment in her voice as she offered me her deepest condolences. She told me, "This is the call that I never wanted to receive."

The coroner and the funeral director came by later. I didn't want my family to see them take Beth's body out on the gurney. I told Kirstyn, Kelsey, and Elaine to stay with me on the deck when they did. I remember thinking that it was ironic how Bryan Law dropped everything to build the ramp, and we only used it a couple of times. They wheeled her over it the day she came home from the hospital. They wheeled her out to take her for her platelets the next day, and wheeled her back up when she returned home. And now they would wheel her out of the house and down that ramp one last time.

My neighbor, Dana Poirier, came out onto the deck later that afternoon. She told me she had someone that I needed to meet. I came inside, and she introduced me to James Terry, the owner of the James Terry Funeral Home, which I had called a couple of days earlier. He was incredibly kind and sympathetic. He handed me his card and said that I should come to the funeral home the next day, and he would help me begin the process of planning the funeral. He asked me if I had a cemetery plot and gave me information for the first of many difficult decisions I would be making. I recognized the name of one of the cemeteries, Northwood. It was in a perfect location between my home and my church. Jim said he could arrange for me to pick out a plot the following day.

I wrote the hardest post that I ever had to write that evening informing my Facebook followers that Beth had gone to her heavenly home. An outpouring of love began immediately. Thousands of responses poured in from people around the world who offered their prayers and support to my family. It was overwhelming. I couldn't read all the comments, but I did my best to read as many as I could. **If you were one of those people who wrote me, thank you from the bottom of my heart. Your support and prayers meant the world to my family and me.**

My phone began ringing with calls of concern and support from family and friends around the country. Brian and Roy prepared a nice meal for everyone. I realized I had to stop answering the phone so that I could sit and eat. I hadn't had a chance to sit at my dining room table and enjoy a meal for several months. Now that I was able to, the most important member of our family was missing.

Our dear friends, Mark and Mary Beth Roe, came by after dinner. They are both so kind and caring. They gave my family and me big hugs and expressed their sadness over the loss of Beth. I introduced them to everyone who was in the house. They also had come by the day that my dad passed away over nineteen years earlier. They are the type of friends who show up when you need them. My family had been close to the Roes since we first met them in Minneapolis in 1988 when Mary Beth and I were hosts on CVN. Mary Beth was very close with Beth.

Jeff came over with Cole and Gavin shortly after Mark and Mary Beth arrived. Kirstyn and Jeff took Cole upstairs and told him that his Gam had gone to heaven. That little boy let out a wail and cried very loud and for a very long time. When they came downstairs, he came right up to me and gave me the biggest hug. A few days before, he had told me that he didn't know what he would do if Gam left us and went to see Jesus. I said he could always come see me when he missed her, and we could talk about her. He told me how sad he was and how much he missed her already. I told him that I felt the same way and that we would help each other get through it.

It wasn't long after I crawled into bed that night that Kelsey knocked on my door. She came in and asked if she could sleep in the bed with me. I said, "Of course you can Kelsey!" She wanted to talk so we talked. She told me she was angry that her mom was gone—and sad that Beth wouldn't be at her wedding when she got married. She wouldn't be there when she had children to help her and give her advice. "I don't understand dad!" she cried out.

I hugged her and said, "I don't either Kelsey, but we have to believe that God has a purpose and a plan for us."

As I finally started to fall asleep, Kelsey asked, "Daddy are you going to leave?"

I said, "Kelsey I might be doing some traveling in the future, but if I go anywhere you can always come with me."

"No daddy. Are you going to die?" she said through her tears.

"No Kelsey! I'm not. If I tried to go to heaven, mommy would tell me to get back down here and finish the job. She would tell me that I needed to be here for you, Kirstyn, Cole, Gavin and Jeff!" I responded. That answer must have satisfied her because it wasn't long after that we both fell asleep.

29

Planning a Celebration

I had grown so used to not sleeping that by 5:30 the next morning, I was wide- awake. I got out of bed and walked into the kitchen. When I turned on the coffee machine, I had an emotional meltdown. I started weeping uncontrollably. I had brought Beth her coffee every morning for many years, and it hit me hard that I would never be able to bring her coffee again.

Brian was sleeping on the couch in the living room. He woke up and came out into the kitchen. He put his arms around me and did his best to console me. We talked for a while, and then we decided that we would go to Kelly's for breakfast.

Beth loved eating breakfast at Kelly's. We knew all the people who worked there. All of the waitresses offered me their condolences. They all came over to our table and gave me hugs. I sat facing the door, and every time I looked at it, I expected to see Cakies walk in. I wanted to feel close to her, so I ordered what she always ordered: two eggs over easy, bacon, rye toast and, of course, coffee. Thus began my first day on earth without Beth.

Our next stop was the cemetery where I had to pick out a plot. It was another beautiful October day. I had passed by this particular cemetery many times but had never driven in to see its general appearance. It dates back to the early 1700's and sits on a hill overlooking the town. It is nestled among many tall maple and oak trees, and on this late October morning, the trees looked as if they were on fire from the gorgeous colors of fall foliage. The array of red, oranges, yellows, —it was dazzling. As I pulled my car through the entrance and saw the headstones, I felt a wave of fear sweep over me. I told Brian that I was having a panic attack. The realization that I was there to pick out a plot for Beth was overwhelming. *Was I really picking out a place to bury Beth? She was my life partner for almost thirty-seven years!* It seemed like a bad dream. It was surreal to be shopping for her gravesite.

Brian helped calm me down. Ron, the gentleman that we were supposed to meet, came walking up to my car. He was in charge of the cemetery, but it seemed like he was also the groundskeeper. He told us a little bit of the history of the cemetery and explained how the town founders had set this piece of land apart because of the tranquil setting. He took us to a place that he said was the best plot he had available. It was situated directly under a massive oak tree facing east. The morning sun filtered through the branches and leaves of the oak tree and gave an almost magical feeling to the spot. I knew right away that this was where Beth should be buried. It seemed as if she whispered in my ear, "This is perfect." I told Ron I wanted to purchase it and the plot next to it so that when my time comes, I can be laid to rest next to her.

We had time to go back to the house to be with family before our early afternoon appointment at the funeral home. My brother-in-law, Ronn, told me we should write Beth's obituary, so we could give it to the funeral home director that afternoon. He explained that they would want to send it out to the local papers and the papers of the towns where Beth and I grew up. Ronn had been through this process many times in his forty years of ministry. He kept track of where I needed to be and when. He knew exactly what needed to be done, and I was fortunate to have him guide me through the process. I asked him to come with me to the funeral home that afternoon to help me with all of the decisions that needed to be made.

Writing Beth's obituary seemed like an impossible task. How do you sum up a life in just a few paragraphs to be printed in the newspaper? Beth was such a big part of our world. We couldn't begin to do her justice with such limited space. We wrote it together with the help of all of our family members who were there. Tears flowed while we worked on it. When we finished and read it back, we were satisfied that we had done our best for such a limited format. Roy typed it up on the computer; another task checked off the list. Many more still needed to be done before the end of the day.

When I look back on this time, I realize I was in a complete fog. At a certain point, I think I detached myself from the process because it was too painful. Picking a cemetery plot for Beth; writing her obituary; picking out a casket, and on and on and on. When the realization of what I was doing fully hit me, I went to pieces. I think the state of fog is a survival technique that numbs you to the reality of it all, and helps you get through it.

Ronn, Brian and I went to the funeral home that afternoon. We were there for several hours. Jim, the director, took me through each decision that had to be made. I remember walking into a room with several types of caskets. I saw one that had a pinkish overtone to it, and I knew that was the one, because Beth loved pink. They showed me eight to ten examples of artwork for the announcement cards and the registry book. When I saw the Thomas Kinkade artwork known as *Bridge of Faith* I knew that was the one.

Beth bought me a Bible back in 1981. On the inside cover page, she wrote, "Dan, You can do two things in your world: you can build a wall, or you can build a bridge. You've helped me build my bridge to Jesus Christ and to others. I've learned that love never fails; it endures all things, and that's the love I have for you. Thank you for sharing Daniel Wheeler with me. Just a simple little thing like loving me brought God into my life. All my Love, Elizabeth Ann, I Corinthians 13:4-8."

When I saw the bridge, I knew it was right. I had worked with Thomas Kinkade many times over the years on QVC. Beth had met him as well as his wife and children. She particularly loved his painting *Bridge of Faith*.

Next, we had to finalize the obituary and include all the details, such as the when and where for both the visitation and Celebration of Life service. I called Pastor Lee Wiggins at our church to figure it all out. I then had to decide which newspapers would receive the obituary for publication. I called Roy and Carol and asked for the names of the local papers where Beth grew up and where her immediate family lived. I also had it sent to my hometown newspaper in St. Joe, Michigan. I had to pick out a photo of Beth to be included in the obituary.

I knew that Beth would want people to support a good cause in place of sending flowers. My niece, Terra, has a daughter named Kendall who has mitochondrial disease. The hospital bills and associated costs have been astronomical. Beth loved Kendall and always followed her progress closely. My daughters and I decided that we should ask people to donate to the Kendall Quinn Medical Fund instead of buying flowers. We included that in the bulletin for the service. Many donated and the money raised was a huge blessing to Terra's family.

Beth had always made us promise that we would bury her in her jammies. She told us that she loved being comfy in life, so she wanted to be buried that way. Kirstyn picked out some cute, cozy jammies for her to wear and dropped them off at the funeral home that morning.

After a couple of hours, we had made all the decisions that were necessary that day. I picked out the casket, the vault, flowers, the announcements, the newspapers, etc. I was fortunate to work with a great funeral home. All of the people I worked with were incredibly kind, compassionate and helpful.

By the end of the day, I was utterly exhausted from all of the decisions and all of the emotions. I had a headache, doubtless because I hadn't eaten a full meal since breakfast. But there were still numerous decisions to be made and tasks to be done. My pastor, Lee Wiggins, had set up a meeting at the church for the next day, following the second Sunday morning service. We also had to return to the funeral home as a family to decide if we wanted the casket to be open or closed.

Let me offer some practical advice to everyone reading this book. Even though none of us wants to think about death, advance planning will relieve a lot of stress. When a loved one dies, it is so incredibly difficult emotionally. But then you have to make so many decisions so quickly that it is entirely overwhelming. If you or your loved one have plans to be buried, buy a plot in advance. Think about the funeral home that you will use. Think about what the service will look like. Save you and your loved ones a lot of extra stress and emotional strain by making some of those decisions in advance. Some funeral homes offer a complete package in advance so that when the inevitable happens everything is in place.

We came home to grab a bite; then I took Brian to the mall to buy him a suit to wear for the visitation and the service. We had to find one quickly, and we needed it tailored and ready for pick up by early afternoon on Monday; the visitation would be that evening.

On the way to the mall, I called Pastor Lee again. We had attended Calvary Fellowship in Downingtown, Pennsylvania, (aka CF Downingtown), for over twenty years. I had been in contact with Lee about Beth's viewing and service. He was accommodating and prepared; he had stayed in close touch with me during the final days of Beth's illness. In fact, he came all the way down to Philadelphia and visited Beth one afternoon during her last week in the big hospital there. The three of us had a great visit in Beth's hospital room. He told me that the church was going to try and stream Beth's service live on the Internet so that friends and family around the country could watch it. This would be the first time the church ever live streamed a service.

Brian found the perfect suit, and it could be ready at 1 p.m. on Monday. By the time we got home that evening, we were all exhausted. Even though we had made many decisions, there was still a lot to be done before the visitation on Monday evening.

When we got home, my mom, Marge, and brother-in-law, George, had just arrived after a very long drive from Wisconsin. My sister, Dawn, and her husband, Glenn Bemis came from Quincy, Illinois, along with two of my close college buddies who also arrived that evening. Terry Steen was my college roommate and teammate on the Evangel College baseball team for four years. He remains one of my closest friends. He came along with another great friend, Scott Laing, who also played baseball with me for four years in college. They flew in from Tampa, Florida. Thankfully, our neighbors, the Poiriers opened up their home for our family and friends. We filled both houses and some hotel rooms with people who came from all over the country to celebrate Beth's life.

At dinner that evening, I shared some of the miracles I had seen during Beth's battle. Noelle shared a miracle of her own. She told us that she and her husband Nate were looking at the calendar a year earlier to plan their vacations for the year. Nate had two weeks of vacation available. One of their holidays was already planned, but they didn't know which other week to take. They randomly picked this week, which allowed Noelle to be with us to say goodbye to her Aunt Beth. And, as I mentioned earlier, she and Terra got the last two seats on the plane to come to Pennsylvania for their goodbye visit. Some would call those "coincidences," but I call them "miracles." God knew.

When I woke up on Sunday, the realization that Beth was gone hit me full force. I cried again at the coffee maker, and I cried with every sip of my coffee. Morning coffee was never going to be the same without Beth.

Ronn, Brian and I met with Pastor Lee, his wife Anne, and the other folks who would be involved in Beth's service. Ronn and I had talked about how the service should go. Since he and Pastor Lee had done hundreds of funeral services, it didn't take long to plan out the order of the Celebration of Beth's Life. Anne Wiggins put together the program for the service, so we finalized those details as well. I told the music minister that Beth's favorite hymns and choruses were, "How Great Thou Art", "Amazing Grace" and "Victory in Jesus." We also arranged a time for Alyssa to rehearse her song with the musicians. I had asked her to sing a song that Beth loved, "I Know My Redeemer Lives."

Kirstyn, Kelsey, Elaine, and I went to the funeral home that afternoon. Jim Terry told us we needed to see Beth and decide if we wanted an open or closed casket. We walked into the room where she was, and we barely took two steps when Kirstyn, Kelsey and I said in unison, "Closed!" It was an easy and unanimous decision. The shell left behind wasn't Beth. As hard as the makeup people at the funeral home had tried, they couldn't match her smile. She didn't look right, and we didn't want to remember her that way. Before we left we put some drawings and notes from Cole and Gavin in the casket with her.

My sister, Dawn, and her husband, Glenn Bemis, arrived late in the afternoon from Quincy, Illinois. That evening I had to stop at the grocery store—everyone in that store knew Beth because she always talked to everyone when she shopped. Brian and Glenn were with me. I wasn't inside the store for two minutes when I completely broke down again. I bent over and started weeping out loud. I glanced at the pharmacy where I had picked up drugs for Beth several times a week for the past three years, and it hit me that I would never pick up medications for her again. The store started spinning on me, and I could barely breathe. I handed Brian the list of what we needed and Glenn helped me walk out to the car. He had to hold me up because I couldn't even walk on my own. My world wasn't right without Beth, and I couldn't make the tears stop.

Grief hits you like a wave. There is no predicting when or where it will strike. It comes out of nowhere. It hit me again several times while I was writing this book.

Monday, November 2nd, 2015, was another hectic day. Beth's visitation was scheduled for that evening from five o'clock to eight o'clock. My college buddies and I went back to Kelly's for breakfast. They tried to get my mind off of things by sharing funny stories from our college days. They gave me a lot of support and comfort. It meant a lot to me that they were there.

Oscar, my friend who was creating the video for Beth's service, asked me to stop by his house to see the rough cut. Five seconds into the recording, I was crying like a baby. He did a great job. I suggested a few minor changes and asked if he could come by the church and have some of the pictures of Beth playing on the big screens, so people would have something to look at while they stood in line for the visitation. He said he would be there. I had a very clear picture in my head of how I wanted Beth's video to end, so I told Oscar what I wanted, and he executed it beautifully. We had a picture of Kirstyn, Kelsey and Beth's left wrists with the tattoos that spelled faith, hope and love. I wanted to dissolve from that to the sign that Dana made saying, "Welcome Home Beth," and then the shot of the oak tree where she would be buried. I then wanted her name with her birth date and the date of her birth to eternal life underneath. The music would then fade out and we would add the last message she recorded on my phone when she said, "I love you so much. I love you guys so much. You're in my heart, and I'm in yours forever, forever and ever." Oscar edited it all together beautifully.

30

A Celebration of Beth's Life

When we showed up at the church for the visitation, people were already starting to arrive. I was met by a good friend of mine named Joe LaSpina, as soon as I walked in the door. Joe couldn't stay, but he wanted to give me his condolences and a big hug.

Inside, I passed by many large photos of Beth mounted to black poster boards sitting on easels. They lined the hallway leading into the sanctuary. My nieces, Terra and Noelle, are both photographers. They wanted to do something special for the service, so they went through boxes of old pictures and photo CD's and picked out the best ones of Beth and had them blown up and mounted. That was such a pleasant surprise for me. I had no idea they were going to do that for us. The cover photo for this book was my favorite and I have a copy of that photo in my home office.

Our family gathered in front of the casket to get ready to greet all of the friends who came out to pay their respects. I had told Jim Terry that our grandsons called Beth "Gam." So he had a covering made for the top of the casket that had "Gam" embroidered on it. Kirstyn told me when she saw it laying on Beth's casket she just started crying. It touched her heart.

Hundreds of people showed up for the visitation. They let them come into the sanctuary at 5 p.m., and the line stayed long and steady until after 8 p.m. My daughters, Beth's family, and I were all in that fog-like state. For some reason, I was able to talk with people without breaking down. Of course, we all handle grief in different ways. Because I talk for a living, I talked. Ronn kept watching the time and watching the line of people. Periodically he had to remind me to talk less so we could get through the line.

So many dear friends of our family came. Many of my co-workers from QVC were there, including hosts past and present, producers, directors, studio personnel, members of the Talent department, buyers, vendors and executives. Many of my daughters' friends and parents came, along with some of their former teachers and coaches. There were even friends of Beth's whom I had never met! We all felt supported by the love of so many. Beth was greatly loved because she loved greatly.

We woke up to another glorious fall day on Tuesday, November 3rd. It seemed like God was celebrating Beth's life along with us. This was the day we would commemorate her life and then lay her body to rest.

Our family all gathered in the green room of the church with Pastor Lee, Ronn, and the musicians. We prayed and then entered the church. There were several hundred people in the sanctuary, and thousands around the country who watched the live stream on their computers, thanks to the work of Peter Bruner who was in charge of the tech work at the church.

The service was beautiful. Reverend Lee Wiggins did a great job with the opening and closing remarks. Alyssa Boyd sang "I Know My Redeemer Lives". She didn't just sing the song; she ministered to everyone through it. Her voice was powerful and filled with emotion. I know it was a challenge for her to get through that song, knowing how much she loved Beth. This was probably the most challenging message that

Ronn ever delivered. Beth was his sister-in-law for thirty-one years; she was family...he loved her as much as we all did. His voice quivered a couple of times, but he did an amazing job of communicating who Beth Wheeler was. He interjected humor and wove in many personal stories about her.

Unlike some funerals I have attended, this one communicated who Beth was on a very personal level and the powerful impact that her life had on so many people. The video presentation that Oscar Dovale put together was perfect. I am so thankful to Oscar for all of the hours he put into it. It was indeed a labor of love. My daughter, Kelsey, picked out the two songs: "I Will See You Again" by Carrie Underwood and "Dancing with the Angels" by Monk & Neagle. They could not have been any more perfect. The service was beautiful. It was meaningful. It was memorable. Just like Beth.

I heard from hundreds of people around the country who were deeply moved by this service. Many said that if Ronn were the pastor of a church within a hundred mile radius of where they lived, they would attend it.

The service was a true Celebration of the Life of Elizabeth Ann Wheeler. You can watch it on YouTube under *Beth Wheeler Memorial Service-A Celebration of Life*. It will give you a chance to learn more about her.

Following the church service, we gathered at her gravesite to say our final goodbyes. Our family hugged and kissed her casket. I remember watching Cole and Gavin kissing the casket and listening as they each said, "I love you, Gam." I looked at my son-in-law, Jeff, and our two beautiful daughters, Kirstyn and Kelsey. Our hearts were all breaking together. But I knew we would stay close and carry on the way Beth wanted us to.

After Ronn finished his message, James Terry, the owner of the James J. Terry Funeral Home, said he would like to say a few words. He told everyone gathered that it was a real honor for his team to provide the services for Beth. He praised our family and Ronn and Lee for the beautiful ceremony. He said that the love of our family deeply touched him and that this was one of the most memorable and meaningful services he could remember. He told us that he knew Beth was an exceptional lady from all of the stories he had heard from the many people who were touched so deeply by her life. His words meant so much to us that day.

Later that afternoon, family and friends gathered at Dana and Steve Poirier's home. They decided they wanted to hold a Celebration Party for Beth after the service. It was very thoughtful, and it gave us a chance to gather and honor Beth one more time.

One of my lifelong friends, Joel Kruggel, drove all the way from New Hampshire to attend Beth's service. I had no idea he would be there, but it meant a great deal to me that he came. He knew Beth very well from when we first started dating and attended Joel's church in Bolingbrook, Illinois. Joel was the very first friend I remember having. We'd been the closest of friends for many years. We had a chance to catch up at the party, and then I was able to show him our house- the one that Beth made into a home.

31

The Birth of Fearless Faith

The day after Beth's service, Kelsey was looking at Beth's cell phone, which she found on the nightstand by our bed. She started going through her messages and, to her surprise, she found a text that Beth had written to her but had never sent. Kelsey posted on her Facebook page that finding that message was an unexpected blessing to her. She felt like her mama was still sending her messages from heaven.

During the final year of Beth's life, I began to feel like I was receiving a message from heaven. I didn't hear an audible voice, but I felt in my spirit that God was giving us a story that I was supposed to tell. Two months after Beth passed, I started writing blogs about our journey on my QVC Facebook page. They became quite popular, and many of the readers said that I should write a book about her life and the brave way in which she faced death. I also felt like I was supposed to travel around and speak publicly about our journey. As I prayed about it, I felt like God was leading me into full-time ministry. I knew I needed help, so I looked to my two best friends.

Brian Roland and Terry Steen came to support me when Beth was dying. They both decided to stay for the entire week after her service. They knew that it would hit me hard after all of our friends and family left. Two days after Beth's service, I began to share with them that I believed God was leading me into ministry. I took them out for lunch on that Friday. As we sat down at our table, I said, "Guys, I feel like I have done very little for the Lord during my lifetime. Now that I'm 61 years of age, it's time to do something significant. I don't want to retire to the golf course. I want to use these years to make an impact for the Lord and to honor Beth's life and memory."

Brian and Terry immediately told me that they wanted to help me accomplish that. We formed the idea for what is now Fearless Faith Ministries that day over lunch. We chose the name because Beth had faced death fearlessly.

Today, we have a relatively large following on our Facebook page @FFM60. The name of the page is Fearless Faith Ministries. The three of us take turns delivering three-minute messages every morning. We call these messages "Your Morning Cup of Inspiration." Fearless Faith is a nonprofit 501(c) 3 corporation. A portion of the proceeds from this book will help us continue to minister in exciting new ways, as do the donations from our supporters and followers. God continues to open other doors of ministry to us, including radio and television.

Our primary goal is to point people to Jesus. We believe that He is the answer to the problems that plague humanity today. We are not about religion. Jesus condemned the religious leaders of his time for their hypocrisy. He said they were "whited sepulchers," meaning that they were all cleaned up on the outside, but they were dead on the inside. Fearless Faith is about spreading the gospel, or the Good News, that we can have a relationship with God. Our central message is that anyone can have eternal life by simply asking God to forgive their sins and by accepting the gift of atonement that Jesus provided through his death and resurrection. We believe that Jesus is **the way, the truth and the life**" as He said in **John 14:6, King James Version of the Bible.**

Fearless Faith is also about inspiring the Baby Boomer generation not to retire to a life of leisure, but to use their retirement years to accomplish something for God. Too many people retire, and then die shortly afterward, because they don't have a reason to get out of bed in the morning. Living a life of Fearless Faith means your retirement years can be the most exciting and productive of your entire life. We want to use the resources God has given us during our working years to give back and inspire people to make these the best years of their life.

As I look back and see what God has done since Beth went to heaven, I realize that His ways are higher than our ways. Fearless Faith Ministries and this book are just the beginning of what I believe God is going to do because of Beth's passing. We don't understand why supposedly "bad things" happen, but if we put our trust in God He can work through every situation to accomplish great things. He has already done that, and I can only imagine what He is going to do in the future.

If you would like to learn more about Fearless Faith Ministries, please check out our website @www.ffaith. org. You can also join us on Facebook @FFM60 or @ fearlessfaithministries on Instagram. Feel free to connect with me at any of those places.

32

Good Grief

When someone you love dies, your grief runs deep. I remember looking out the window the morning after Beth passed away. I saw cars driving by on the road, and I became angry because I realized that for most people it was just another day. For most people, it was life as usual. But it wasn't for my family. Our world had come to a halt because our anchorperson, the matriarch of our family, had died. She was our world, but the rest of the world was unaware that anything had changed.

I think everyone who loses a loved one experiences this. Because you feel sad and lonely, you want the rest of the world to feel the same. But they don't. They just go on with their lives.

The weeks that followed after Beth passed were brutal. I was all right while Brian and Terry were with me, but after that, I turned into a hermit. I didn't want to see anybody or go anywhere. Taking a shower and getting dressed was too much work. Most days I stayed in the house, looked at pictures and watched videos of Beth and cried. I cried for hours upon end.

I received a beautiful sympathy card in the mail that was signed by all the nurses and nursing assistants who cared for Beth during her final weeks at the big hospital in Philadelphia. One of the nurses named Stephanie was particularly fond of

Beth. She bonded with Beth and Kirstyn. Since Kirstyn is also a nurse they had a lot in common. Stephanie was one of the nurses who always came in early to try to get Beth as one of her patients each day. She wrote in the card, "Beth Wheeler helped me rediscover why I went into nursing in the first place." That card just tore me up emotionally. I couldn't stop crying after I read it. This was yet another example of the impact Beth made on the lives of everyone around her.

Anthony Corrado, my good friend who helped with Beth's surprise party, stopped by the house a few times during those weeks. He would talk to me and listen. He did his best to encourage me that things would get easier with time. He did what a good friend does. He showed up. Just before Thanksgiving, Anthony actually talked me into getting out of the house for an afternoon and evening. Three great friends named Shane Eck, Scott Kranson, and Neil Plotkin all wanted to help me get my mind off my troubles, so we played golf and went to dinner. They helped me laugh, and they helped me enjoy life for a few hours.

Thanksgiving was quickly approaching, so I was about to experience my first "first." The first year after your loved one passes you go through all the firsts (i.e., first Thanksgiving, First Anniversary, First Christmas, etc.) without them. Thanksgiving was brutal. Our family gathered at Ed and Nancy's home. I felt like I was going through the motions. It was just wrong that Beth wasn't there. They left an empty seat at the table in her honor. We all felt her absence strongly. I just wanted to get through the dinner and go home. As we were all walking out to our cars, little two-year-old Gavin looked up at the night sky and said, "Hi Gam. We miss you!"

Next up on my calendar of "firsts" was our wedding anniversary on December 22nd. It would have been our thirty-first. Kirstyn suggested that we go somewhere as a family so that I wouldn't just sit in the house and cry. We decided to go to New York City to see the musical *The Lion King*. We found a good deal on some hotel rooms near Broadway and spent two days and a night. We had fun and bonded as a family. Beth was on all of our minds. I kept picturing her there with us as we dined at Ellen's Stardust Diner, climbed the Empire State Building, looked at all of the Christmas decorations, walked down Broadway and watched the musical.

I knew Christmas was going to be the most difficult of all. Every Christmas song reminded me of Beth. I didn't want to hear any Christmas music. I didn't want to sing any carols, and I had no desire at all to decorate. I didn't even want to put up a tree. In short, I just didn't want to celebrate Christmas. Kirstyn and Kelsey kept telling me that Mom would want us to celebrate it. They insisted that we put up the tree and decorate. They turned on Christmas music, and I just started crying. Every song reminded me of Beth. Every ornament we put on the tree made me sad because each one had a memory tied to it that involved Cakies. It just didn't seem like Christmas without her, and I didn't *want* it to be Christmas, because she wasn't here. Beth always bought us all Christmas Pajamas that we opened on Christmas Eve after we came home from church. Our girls found theirs unwrapped in Beth's closet. We took a picture of them wearing the pajamas in front of the Christmas tree and they posted it on social media with a caption that thanked their mom for thinking about them even in heaven.

Beth's birthday was in early February, so it seemed like the parade of "firsts" would never end. Our family went to Kelly's and ordered what Beth always ordered. We got purple (her favorite color) helium balloons and wrote messages to her on them with marker pens. There was freezing rain that day, so none of our balloons made it up to heaven the way we intended. I'm sure our efforts gave her a good laugh.

The "firsts" kept coming, but at least we had a little break between her birthday and Easter. I had gone back to work and started hosting QVC shows again in late November. I co-hosted my first show back with my good buddy Dan Hughes. During my twenty-nine years with QVC, people always confused Dan and me. Could it have been because we were both short, bald, from the Midwest and named Dan? It was a running joke with us. We often got each other's mail, emails, and texts. Before coming to QVC, Dan was a comedian. He's a hilarious guy off camera and always kept me laughing. He was the perfect guy to have next to me as I ventured back in front of the cameras. His humor and his attitude got me through that first show. Getting back to work, in general, was a big help. It was better than staying home and crying all the time.

When you lose someone you love, be prepared. There is no getting around the year of firsts. All you can do is make it through. The good news is that the year of seconds is a little bit better. The holidays, birthdays and anniversaries are always tough, but they do become more bearable with time.

Our hospice organization offered grief counseling, so I decided that I would take advantage of it. I'd had counseling in the past, but I never really felt like it helped me very much. The minute I met this counselor, however, I knew I had found someone who would help. She was empathetic and caring. I was dealing with so much sadness and guilt. I have talked to several people who have lost spouses, and they all experienced the same feelings. They all struggled with guilt for being the one who lived. I remember asking God why Beth got cancer and died and not me. I felt like it should have been me, not Beth. Instead of remembering all the things I did right as her husband, my mind kept focusing on the things I did wrong. One day the counselor said something that really inspired me. She said, "Dan, you need to realize that Beth is in heaven with God, and they are not judging you, they are both cheering you on! They want you to finish your race and live your life to the fullest!" That really connected with me. Picturing Beth in heaven cheering for me turned my attitude around. I decided that I did need to finish the race, and that was the best way to honor her memory. I felt like a thousand pounds were lifted off my shoulders.

I did more grief counseling, and joined a group for recently widowed people. I attended eight sessions, and they were very helpful. There were about a dozen people in the class, and we all helped each other through a very tough time.

If you have lost a loved one, don't be afraid to seek out grief counseling. And: remember the good times. Remember the best things about your relationship. Don't beat yourself up over mistakes you made. Realize that your departed loved one is cheering you on. They want you to keep living and to finish your race strong!

33

A Gift From Above

After Beth passed, we decided that we would take a family vacation to a warm climate, during March the following year. We found a beautiful family resort on Captiva Island in the Gulf of Mexico. Kelsey, Kirstyn, Jeff, Gavin, Cole, and I flew down and spent a relaxing, rejuvenating week in the warm Florida sunshine during the second week of March.

While we were there, Kirstyn informed us that she was pregnant. We were all excited, and talked about how great it would be if she had a girl. She said that she would name the girl, Brooke Elizabeth, in honor of her mom. Kirstyn's middle name is Brooke and Beth's full name was Elizabeth. We tried not to get our hopes too high, since her first two babies were boys, and they are fantastic. It just seemed like a girl at this time would complete the circle of life.

We arrived back home on a Saturday afternoon, and Kirstyn had invited Kelsey and me to attend a banquet for a running group she belonged to that raised money for cancer. She had been asked to speak about her mom's battle with cancer, and was nervous that she would break down emotionally. Not sure she could get through it, she wanted us there for support. Sure enough, as soon as she introduced herself, she started crying. I thought, "Oh no. There is no way she will get through this." Kelsey and I prayed hard. Miraculously, Kirstyn pulled it together and did an excellent job. Her talk was powerful. She spoke straight from the heart, and it touched the hearts of everyone who heard her.

Brian, Terry and I began working on Fearless Faith Ministries during the next few months. We started posting our three- minute "Morning Cups of Inspiration" on Facebook, and slowly but surely we built a following. A lot of people began responding to our messages. Many wrote us to say that our ministry was helping them grow in their faith, and that they enjoyed starting every day with their "Morning Cup of Inspiration." It didn't take long to realize that we were moving in the right direction. God had begun something because we responded to His leading.

I continued to work as a host for QVC, and was glad that I had a great job that I loved, and that I worked for one of the best companies on earth.

Easter brought another problematic "first," as did Kirstyn and Kelsey's birthdays. Of course, Mother's Day was an even bigger challenge, especially for Kirstyn and Kelsey. As summer began, we all realized more and more that Beth wanted us to keep moving forward with our lives. She wanted us all to finish our race. We got together many times that summer and always talked about her. She especially loved summer days by the pool. In fact, she referred to our backyard and pool area as "our little piece of heaven." This was our first summer without her. I was despondent when I opened the pool that year because Beth always celebrated the return of summer when that happened.

September eventually came, and Kirstyn's pregnancy progressed nicely. She was due in October, so we began to anticipate the baby's arrival. One day I received a surprising text from Kirstyn while I was at QVC. She informed me that she might have the baby later that day. I wasn't scheduled to be on the air that evening, and I only had one more meeting scheduled that afternoon. I wrote her back and told her that I would meet Kelsey at home after my meeting, and we would meet her and Jeff at the hospital.

As I finished sending the text, I looked at the date on my phone. I couldn't believe my eyes! It was September 21st, the day I met Beth. Our song was always "September" by Earth, Wind and Fire. The first line of that song says, "Do you remember the twenty-first night of September?" It was the song that Beth and I came out dancing to when they introduced us at Kirstyn's wedding reception. I remember silently praying and asking, "Are you going to bring us this baby on this date which was so special to Beth and me? Would you do that for me God?" Then I thought how awesome it would be if Kirstyn had a girl born on this day!

When Kelsey and I walked into Kirstyn's hospital room later that afternoon, she told us she probably wouldn't be having the baby until much later in the evening. She said we should go out for dinner in West Chester, and bring some food back for Jeff and the boys. We thought that was a good idea, so we went to a lovely outdoor café about a mile away. Not long after the waitress brought us our food, I received a text from Jeff telling me that things were progressing quickly and that we should come back to the hospital as soon as possible.

I quickly paid the bill, and drove back as fast as I could. By the time we got up to Kirstyn's floor, the doctor was getting ready to deliver the baby. Kirstyn wanted Kelsey to stay with her during the delivery, so I went to the waiting room alone. Kirstyn had two knit baby hats. One was pink, and one was blue. She gave the hats to Cole, and instructed him to bring the appropriate hat to me in the waiting room after the baby was born. Kelsey came out and joined me shortly after the doctor delivered the baby. I was on pins and needles. She told me the length and the weight of the baby, but she would not tell me or even give me the slightest hint as to whether it was a boy or a girl.

The anticipation was driving me crazy. I was trying hard not to get my hopes too high that it was a girl. Finally, little Cole came through the door and pulled out----------a PINK cap!!!! I about jumped through the roof! I was more excited than I have ever been at a sporting event of any kind. I remember holding that cap, and thanking the Lord for such a wonderful gift to our family. Sweet little Brooke Elizabeth was born at 8:09 p.m. on the twenty-first night of September 2016.

When God gives us a gift, He knows how to do it in a meaningful, miraculous way. Kirstyn wasn't due until October, but God thought it would be pretty cool to have Brooke Elizabeth enter our world on a date that was so meaningful and so personal to Beth and me.

I went into the room, and held that precious baby. I felt like it was thirty years earlier when I held Kirstyn for the first time. She looked just like her mom, with lots of dark hair and big, wide, open eyes. I sensed that Beth was looking down from heaven, and celebrating the moment with us. I have to believe she knew all about Brooke Elizabeth before we did.

Whenever I see my daughters or my grandchildren, I always think of Beth. She was the best mom and the best Gam ever. Cole, Gavin and I talk of her often, and we always say that she gave the best hugs. She knew how to say, "I love you" with a hug. On the day that Brooke Elizabeth was born, God gave us all an extra tight hug just the way that Beth always did. He told us that He still loves us, and He will never leave us. Whenever I see little Brooke, I see Beth.

Even though she had to leave us physically, we still feel Beth's love every day. It is a powerful love. It's like a hurricane. It hits everyone in its path.

"Every good gift and every perfect gift is from above and cometh down from the Father of lights, with whom there is no variableness, neither shadow of turning."
James 1:17, The King James Version of the Bible

Grandkids, L to R: Cole Daniel, Brooke Elizabeth and Gavin Tayler-2017.

Afterword

After writing this book, I asked my daughters to add their reflections on their mom's life and passing. I am very grateful to them for honoring their mom with their writing. Following these heart-felt tributes from Kirstyn and Kelsey, you will also find the tribute Beth's sister Carol posted the day after we lost Beth ... Each of these, in its own way, shows the impact of the *hurricane of love* that defined Beth Wheeler. Thank you for taking the time to get to know her. I hope her story has touched your heart and given you hope.

A Soul Mate's Tribute

By Kirstyn Wheeler Hauser

I have never liked the term "soul mates" when it comes to a romantic relationship. I don't believe there is only one person for whom each soul is destined. But in a more nuanced way, my mom and I were "soul mates." She was *my person.* It felt like we were made for each other, and God knew our souls were happiest when we were together. We loved spending time together whether we were going to garage sales, antique stores, lunch, sitting by the pool, or just sitting on the couch watching TV. It didn't matter what we were doing, as long as we were together, we were happy.

For as long as I can remember, my mom and I had a unique mother-daughter relationship. I never went through the usual teenage phase where you think your mom is uncool or is out to ruin your life. In fact, it was just the opposite. I remember friends calling me on a Friday or Saturday night in middle school or high school and asking me if I wanted to hang out. A lot of times, I would politely tell them: thank you so much for asking, but I was going to hang out with my mom. Without fail, my friend would respond: "Can I come with you guys?" My friends loved to be around my mom, and many of them felt closer to her than their own mothers. I can't tell you how many people considered her their "second mom."

My mom somehow had the perfect balance of being my friend, but also being my mother. It's not a balance most people can find. Now that I am a mom myself, I desperately want to see that perfect balance with my kids. I asked her several times what her secret was. How did she become my closest friend and still teach me to respect and honor her as my mother? She always told me that she didn't know, and she didn't have a magic answer. She said we just "clicked."

My mom taught me so much in our short 29 years together. I feel grateful to have had her as long as I did, but sometimes I still feel like we got cheated. She had so much more wisdom to pass along, life lessons to help me learn, failures to help me overcome. What I wouldn't give to have one more day with her one more week, a month, a year or even 10 years. The truth is, no amount of time would have been enough, because without her, a piece of my heart will be forever missing. But in our 29 years together, I believe she taught me everything I need to know to get me through the rest of my life without her physically by my side.

- She taught me to treat everyone I meet with kindness and respect. She was the type of person who made friends with everyone— from the housekeepers in the hospital to the CEO, and treated them all equally.
- She taught me never to judge someone by their past, and to get to know their heart. This way you can find the good in everyone.
- My mom taught me that life is too short, and we don't need to sweat the small stuff.
- Most importantly, she taught me how to be a mother myself. My husband and I lived with my mom and dad for the first year of our elder son's life. I am so thankful for that time, because I learned so much from Mom. I remember when Jeff and I rented an apartment (only 10 minutes from my mom and dad's house), before we

moved out, my mom and I cried every day for a month. Even though we were going to be so close, we couldn't stand the thought of being apart!

I am so happy that my mom got to be a Gam to two of my three kids. My boys loved her so much, but it still breaks my heart that she never got to meet her granddaughter. I know she would have loved her like no other, and spoiled her rotten with kisses and hugs. She was the best Gam. One of my favorite memories is when I would pick my kids up after she babysat them. When I picked them up to give them a hug, I always distinctly remember that the first thing I noticed was: they smelled like her perfume. It always made me smile because I knew they were snuggled and loved all day by her while I was gone. I want to make sure they remember their Gam, so we talk about her often. One of the things they say the most is that their Gam gave "the best hugs ever," and they are right!

The truth is, I could write my own book about all the things I learned from my mom, and what I loved most about her, but I am going to keep this short. What I want you to walk away knowing is that my mom was my favorite person in the world. I will forever be grateful that God chose to put us together. She made everyone's lives better, just by being there. I have no regrets when it comes to my relationship with my mom; we enjoyed our time together, and she always knew how much I loved her, and how much she meant to me. I hope to pass along all the lessons she taught me to my own kids over the years.

A lot of people idolize celebrities or sports heroes, but for me, my mom was my idol. I want to be just like her in so many ways. When people tell me I remind them of my mom, or I sound just like her, it is the best compliment I can receive. She was not only my mom, but my best friend too, and I know that not a day will go by that I don't miss her and feel her absence. But because of her love and the life lessons she taught me, I also know that I will carry her with me for the rest of my life. I cannot wait for the day we get to be reunited again in Heaven, and she scoops me up and gives me one of her big, famous hugs!

Cheering Me On

By Kelsey Wheeler

When my dad asked me to write a tribute to my mom for his book, it took me weeks to bring my fingers to the keyboard. I used to love to write, however, since my mom passed it has been difficult to put my feelings onto paper. I feel as if there are no words that could ever honestly describe how I feel about my mother. Most of the time I do not even know how I feel. Grief is funny. I feel a multitude of emotions in a single day, but when it comes down to processing those emotions I begin to feel… nothing. That is where I stop. I don't go deeper or further. I don't try to dig down into the emotions I felt earlier. I let myself settle for numb. I know it is my mind trying to protect me from the genuine pain living deep inside of me. However, in the long run, I know it is doing more damage than good. Maybe this tribute will be the start of reminding myself that it is okay to feel, to process, and to sit with those emotions for a bit. Please bear with me as I begin to unravel some of my thoughts about my mother.

Ever since I can remember, my mom has been everything to me. She was the beat of my heart and the air that I breathed. She was my protector, my comforter, and my friend. I see the relationship between a mother and a child as one of the most intimate and purest relationships on this earth. My mother loved me before she knew me. I had lived inside of her before I came into this world. She gave me my very life. When I think of the relationship I had with her, I think of Jesus. My relationship with my mother is the closest human relationship I could compare to a relationship with our Creator. Just like Jesus, my mom loved me unconditionally. There is nothing I could have ever done that would keep her from loving me. When I hurt, she hurt. When I rejoiced, she rejoiced. She knew me, she heard me and she saw me. God knew we needed mothers, and I can truly say He blessed me with one of the best.

From a young age, I knew there was something special about her. She was friends with the cashier at our local grocery store, the pharmacist, the bank teller, even the grumpy neighbor behind us…. Everywhere she went she made friends, which is difficult to do when you live on the east coast. My mom grew up in the Midwest, and when she moved here, she said it was one of the most difficult experiences she had ever had. She told me that she was shocked at how rude people were (I'm an east-coast baby—we don't intend to be rude, it is just not the social norm to look or talk to everyone you see). Some people did not respond well to my mother's kindness (I remember my mom smiling and saying hello to a group of girls sitting at a table next to us, and how they immediately looked in the other direction, acting like they didn't hear her), however, that kind of reaction never once stopped her from loving others. I think it made her love on people more.

My mom didn't just say, "Hello, how are you?" You know, that phrase we all say just to be nice and not because we are genuinely interested. My mom would remember people by name; she would ask them questions about their lives, and then she would remember the details the next time she saw them, to continue the conversation. She cared about the lives and hearts of everyone around her, and people knew it.

I grew up with a lot of friends. My house was the place to be. There was always a fully stocked cupboard and a hardy meal for breakfast, lunch, and dinner. There were plenty of cozy blankets and fluffy socks for everyone to have their own. If you looked slightly uncomfortable, or as if there was a little room in your belly for more food, she would make sure you were taken care of. She would never settle for someone sitting on the couch wearing their uncomfortable street clothes, or someone saying they didn't want a second helping for dinner: instead, you would get a pair of sweatpants and a second large plate of food without her even asking you if that's what you wanted. She would treat anyone who was in her home as if they were the most important person. To her they were.

My house was a second home to many of my friends growing up. My mom would let my friends sleep over, not just one night but sometimes, two, or three, nights in a row. Not only did she let them stay during the weekend but during the week as well. When it was time for school, she would pack us lunches and take us to the bus. She would slip my friend and me each some cash, just because. She would give my friends advice about life without ever casting judgment. Many of my friends considered her to be a second mom. Some felt closer to her than they did their own mothers.

Not only was my mom a lover, she was a strong woman who had put up with a lot, especially from me. I was an unruly child (when I say this, people often don't believe me, but ask anyone who knew me as a child, and they would back me up). I put my mom through so much growing up. I was strong willed, and I didn't back down. I had tantrums well into my teenage years— the kind of outburst where one lays on the ground kicking and screaming like a toddler, slamming doors, and yelling, "I hate you!" I once made one of my mom's toughest friends break down in tears when she babysat me for the day.

My sister's bedroom was located furthest from any neighbors' homes, so that's where my mom sent me when I was having my (almost daily) screaming breakdown. She would tell me, "If the neighbors heard you, they would think I was beating you."

When I became a teenager, my mom always somehow knew when I was up to something terrible, and she would call it out before I even stepped a foot out the door. I swear she could read my mind. I couldn't get away with much. Even when I did get away with things, I would tell her what I did. I would have a terrible sense of guilt, and as soon as I told her I would feel much better. She may have yelled at me, but would always, always forgive me. She protected me by keeping all of my secrets from my dad. If he knew half of the things I did, I would have spent all of my high school years grounded, in my room. I remember she once picked me up from my friend's house at 1 a.m. when I had drank too much. I was sick the entire next day, and she covered for me by telling my dad I had the flu.

My mom not only dealt with my strong-willed personality, but she also taught me how to take that personality and turn it into a strength (even though sometimes it still creeps in, negatively). As a child, I struggled with a learning disability and later with severe depression and anxiety. There were days when I did not know if I would make it, both academically and physically. I saw how much my mom fought for me. She fought for me to have the best education and support at school.

As an adult who sometimes attends Individualized Education Plan meetings (for special needs students) for individuals on my caseload, I see how tough IEP meetings can be. A parent needs to know how to advocate for their child properly. My mom fought for me when I felt I couldn't keep living anymore. She kept my heart beating by sitting with me when the anxiety and depression were so intense that she had to hold my arms and legs down to keep me from getting hurt.

For three years straight, she would drive me to and from my therapy sessions an hour there and an hour back. She would tell me how strong I was and how much she believed in me. She kept me moving forward and helped me to fight against the demons and struggles in my life. She had been in the ring along with me the whole time. She was always in my corner. Without my mother, I honestly can say I would not have made it to where I am today. I went on to get a master's degree when the teachers said I most likely wouldn't go to college. My anxiety and depression are now more like inconveniences, because she made sure I learned to manage them by noticing the signs and symptoms, and by using my coping strategies. I believe, of course, they've also faded out as I have grown.

When my mom got sick, I never really believed she would die, despite her being in immense pain. She never complained about the pain. She never asked, "Why me?" Looking back, I think because she did not complain, I didn't realize how bad it was. I never thought it was possible that she would die. To me, my mom always was. So how could she suddenly be no more?

As I am writing this, it has been a little over two and a half years since I have had to live without my mother here. It has been the most terrible thing I have ever been through in my life. I will continue to battle as I go through the stages of my life. I have to continue to deal with the fact and try to find some peace that my mom will not be here physically. She will not be here physically when I get married or have babies. She will not be here physically when I am having a bad day, and I need to hear her voice, or when I need advice. She will not be here to celebrate with me when I am doing something exciting.

Instead, I have to settle for knowing that she is cheering me on from Heaven every step of the way. I have to remember she is still in my corner fighting for me. I have to remind myself that although I will not see her on this side of Heaven again, one day I will be reunited with my mother, and the pain of losing her will not even be a memory.

A Sister's Tribute

By Carol Bellone

I woke up this morning hoping I had a bad dream, but the truth is, my sister died yesterday, and the reality keeps sinking in. Three years ago this month, she was diagnosed with stage 4 uterine cancer. During her sixty-one years, she was a bright light in this crazy world. If you knew Elizabeth Johnson Wheeler, you knew love and life and laughter. It was my privilege to be her big sister, and though I wished we lived closer to each other, I knew that we loved each other to the moon and back, and that the distance was only miles. Her faith was strong, and her love of God brought her peace. She saw glimpses of heaven in her last days and always said she wasn't afraid to die, but she wasn't ready to leave either. During some of my last days with her, I found myself asking her, "How was your day?" and she would say, "I had a great day. It was so much fun to have everyone here." And so faith, hope, and love abide, but the greatest of these is love.

Beth-circa 1980.

Connect with Dan Wheeler at
Fearless Faith Ministries
www.ffaith.org

facebook.com/FFM60/
or www.instagram.com/fearlessfaithministries/

Fearless Faith Ministries
P.O. Box 340008
Tampa, FL 33694

Or
Dan Wheeler Public Figure Page Facebook